The Supposed Mistranslation of
"Homosexual" In 1 Corinthians 6:9

THE 1946
PROJECT

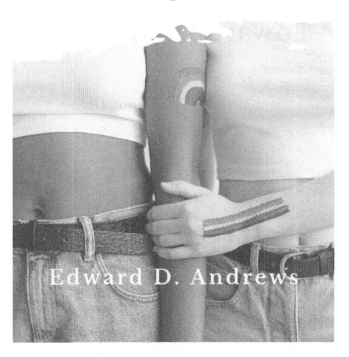

Edward D. Andrews

i

THE 1946 PROJECT
The Supposed Mistranslation of "Homosexual" In 1 Corinthians 6:9

The 1946 Project of the LGBTQ+ Community

Edward D. Andrews

Christian Publishing House

Cambridge, Ohio

Christian Publishing House
Professional Christian Publishing of the Good News!

THE 1946 PROJECT The Supposed Mistranslation of "Homosexual" In 1 Corinthians 6:9 by Christian Publishing House

ISBN-13: 978-1-949586-61-9

ISBN-10: 1-949586-61-8

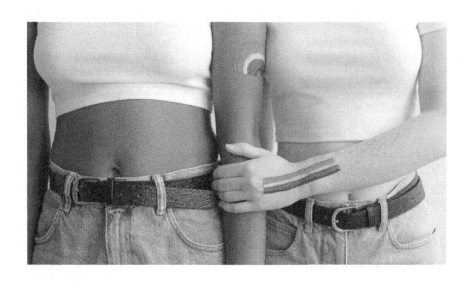

Table of Contents

PREFACE 1

CHAPTER 1 THE 1946 PROJECT The Supposed Mistranslation of "Homosexual" In 1 Corinthians 6:9.................................. 2

Brief History of the Term Homosexual..................................... 5

The Truth about 1 Corinthians 6:9 8

Ungodly People Inexcusable...12

The Bible's Viewpoint of Same-Sex Attraction 26

CHAPTER 2 The Bible's Viewpoint of Homosexuality............30

Human Rebellion Excursion 32

From the Old Person to the New Person 35

What is the Bible's View of Homosexuality?............................38

Genesis 9:18-28 – If it is Ham that saw Noah's nakedness, why is Canaan the one getting cursed? 40

Leviticus 18:22 – Since "Christ is the end of the [Mosaic] law" (Rom. 10:4), does this include homosexuality? 42

The Bible and Sexuality [Excursion] 46

Leviticus 18:22-24 – Is the Curse of Barrenness Behind God's Condemnation of Homosexuality? 48

Why did God Destroy Sodom and Gomorrah? What Was the Sin of Sodom and Gomorrah? 51

Put to Death What Is Earthly in You 56

God's View Homosexuality 57

CHAPTER 3 Explaining the Bible's View of Homosexuality ...60

What is the Bible's View of Homosexuality?............................64

How Should Christians View Homosexuality? 65

Are Christians to Respect Everyone? 65

Is the Christian Stance Not Encouraging Prejudice Against Homosexuals?...66

Did Jesus Teach Tolerance?...66

Is Not Homosexuality Genetically Predisposed? 67

Is It Not Cruel to Tell Those with Same-Sex Attraction to Control Themselves? 68

CHAPTER 4 Avoiding Homosexuality and Controlling Same-Sex Attraction? 73

What Causes Homosexuality 74

God's View of Homosexuality 74

Damage to Us Spiritually 76

10 Empowering Truths For The Same-Sex Attracted Christian 89

Never Give Up 91

CHAPTER 5 Homosexuality – Genes or learned? 93

Genetics of Homosexuality in Men 93

Sons and Daughters of Adam 96

The Origin of Our Troubles...99

CHAPTER 6 How do Christians Handle the Transgender Issue? 101

CHAPTER 7 The Pornography Trap 104

Symptoms and Diagnosis...104

Status as Addiction 106

Online Pornography 106

Breaking the Habit..107

CHAPTER 8 The Self-Abuse of Masturbation 119

The Bible on Masturbation 120

Put to Death Evil Desire 121

Your Thoughts Will Lead You Astray 122

How Does God View our Human Weaknesses?.....................122

CHAPTER 9 Can the Bible Help Us Cope with Loneliness? ..125

The Correct Mindset 125

True Friends 126

We are Never Ever Truly Alone 127

CHAPTER 10 Why has God Permitted Wickedness and
Suffering? 130

    The Issues at Hand 132

    God Settles the Issues 133

    What Have the Results Been? 135

    Was Satan Punished? 136

    Bibliography 139

PREFACE

The claim is that in 1946, theology, history, culture, and politics led to a biblical mistranslation of catastrophic proportions. Supposedly the 1946 movie is a revolutionary documentary that chronicles how the misuse of **a single word in 1 Corinthians 6:9** changed the course of modern history. The 1946 Movie says that their research was "a journey which unveils the mystery of how theology, history, culture, and politics led to a Biblical mistranslation, the man who tried to stop it, and the impassioned academic crusade of the LGBTQIA+ Christian community-**driven to discover the truth**. More than 45,000 churches today still preach that homosexuality is a sin, citing biblical references that condemn "homosexuals." 1946 Movie asks, 'What would change if churches discovered the truth — the word "homosexual" was added to the Bible in 1946 by mistake?' Was it added by mistake? Andrews, author of 170+ books in THE 1946 PROJECT, will investigate this claim and see if the filmmakers **discovered the truth** or **created their own truth**.

Today there are many questions about homosexuality as it relates to the Bible and Christians. What does the Bible say about homosexuality? Does genetics, environment, or traumatic life experiences justify homosexuality? What is God's will for people with same-sex attractions? Does the Bible discriminate against people with same-sex attractions? Is it possible to abstain from homosexual acts? Should not Christians respect all people, regardless of their sexual orientation? Did not Jesus preach tolerance? If so, should not Christians take a permissive view of homosexuality? Does God approve of same-sex marriage? Does God disapprove of homosexuality? If so, how could God tell someone who is attracted to people of the same sex to shun homosexuality? Is that not cruel? If one has same-sex attraction, is it possible to avoid homosexuality? How can I, as a Christian, explain the Bible's view of homosexuality? Christians must always be prepared to reason from the Scriptures, explaining and proving what the Bible does and does not say about homosexuality, yet doing it with gentleness and respect. Andrews will answer these questions and far more.

CHAPTER 1 THE 1946 PROJECT The Supposed Mistranslation of "Homosexual" In 1 Corinthians 6:9

Let's call this the **1946 Project of the LGBTQIA+ Community**. They say that this film will be portraying "A journey which unveils the mystery of how theology, history, culture, and politics led to a Biblical mistranslation, the man who tried to stop it, and the impassioned academic crusade of the LGBTQIA+ Christian community-driven to discover the truth." We will take a moment to consider their comments and then present what the Bible really says. I would preface this with it seems like more of the same; that is, not digging for the truth but rather trying to redefine the truth to fit their ideology and worldview. We have to be open to the idea that the Creator of all things chose the setting, the language, the words, and the time in which the Bible was introduced to humans. It will help us to begin by looking at several literal and semi-literal translations side-by-side. Then, we will look at a brief history of how the term "homosexual" came into existence. That history will expose the 1946 Movie as having a predisposed agenda of not giving their readers and listeners all the facts and even bending the information to fit their narrative. This author does not believe they are genuinely seeking the truth. Lastly, I will over some thoughts in between the sections of their claims.

1 Corinthians 6:9 English Standard Version (ESV)	1 Corinthians 6:9 LEB	1 Corinthians 6:9 New American Standard Bible (NASB 2020)	1 Corinthians 6:9 Revised Standard Version (RSV 1946)	1 Corinthians 6:9 Revised Standard Version (RSV 1971)
⁹ Or do you not know that the unrighteous will not inherit the kingdom of God? Do not be deceived: neither the sexually immoral, nor idolaters, nor	⁹ Or do you not know that the unrighteous will not inherit the kingdom of God? Do not be deceived! Neither sexually immoral people, nor	⁹ Or do you not know that the unrighteous will not inherit the kingdom of God? Do not be deceived;	⁹ Do you not know that the unrighteous will not inherit the kingdom of God? Do not be deceived; neither the immoral,	⁹ Do you not know that the unrighteous will not inherit the kingdom of God? Do not be deceived;

adulterers, nor men who practice homosexuality,	idolaters, nor adulterers, nor passive homosexual partners, nor dominant homosexual partners,	neither the sexually immoral, nor idolaters, nor adulterers, nor homosexuals,	nor idolaters, nor adulterers, nor homosexuals,	neither the immoral, nor idolaters, nor adulterers, nor sexual perverts,

1 Corinthians 6:9 English Revised Version (ERV) 1881 (UK) 9. Or know ye not that the unrighteous shall not inherit the kingdom of God? Be not deceived: neither fornicators, nor idolaters, nor adulterers, nor **effeminate [μαλακοὶ]**, nor **abusers of themselves with men [ἀρσενοκοῖται]**,

1 Corinthians 6:9 American Standard Version (ASV) 1901 [9] Or know ye not that the unrighteous shall not inherit the kingdom of God? Be not deceived: neither fornicators, nor idolaters, nor adulterers, nor **effeminate [μαλακοὶ]**, nor **abusers of themselves with men [ἀρσενοκοῖται]**,

1 Corinthians 6:9 Updated American Standard Version (UASV) [9] Or do you not know that the unrighteous will not inherit the kingdom of God? Do not be deceived; neither fornicators, nor idolaters, nor adulterers, nor **men of passive homosexual acts [μαλακοὶ]**, nor **men of active homosexual acts [ἀρσενοκοῖται]**,[1]

You will notice that the argument from the 1946 project is false based on the 1881 English Revised Version published in Britain and the 1901 American Standard Version and the history of the term "homosexual." You can see two things clearly from these translations before 1946. They say the same thing the new translations are saying but softening their words because of the times. The Bible authors would use a **euphemism,** a mild word substituted for a harsh or direct one that may be found *offensive* or suggest something unpleasant. Or, they say it in a less offensive way of expressing it

---

[1] The two Greek terms refer to passive men partners and active men partners in consensual homosexual acts.

but saying the same thing. Literal translations are word for word and carry those euphemisms over into their translations. An example is sexual relations. In the Bible, the Bible authors in the Old Testament and the New Testament would say that _____ knew _____. This meant that _____ had sexual relations with _____. This was because of the times. Modern interpretive translations do not do this. Let's look at an example of this: Leviticus 18:19.

Dynamic Equivalent Interpretive Translation

Leviticus 18:19 New Living Translation (NLT)

19 "Do not have sexual relations with a woman during her period of menstrual impurity.

Word for Word Literal Translations

Leviticus 18:19 Updated American Standard Version (UASV)

19 "You shall not approach a woman to uncover her nakedness during her menstrual uncleanness.

Leviticus 18:19 American Standard Version (ASV) 1901

19 And thou shalt not approach unto a woman to uncover her nakedness, as long as she is impure by her uncleanness.

Leviticus 18:19 English Revised Standard Version (ERV) 1881

19 "And thou shalt not approach unto a woman to uncover her nakedness, as long as she is impure by her uncleanness.

Notice that what is being talked about is **'sexual relations'** and **'period of menstrual impurity.'** This is where wording says the same thing but is not so plainly but clear enough not to miss the point. Notice too that the older literal translations are saying the same thing: "thou shalt not approach unto a woman to uncover her nakedness, as long as she is impure by her uncleanness."

The **older** pre-1946 literal translations words are apparent, "**effeminate [μαλακοὶ] [soft men]**, nor **abusers of themselves with men [ἀρσενοκοῖται] [liers with men]**," and the newer translations: "men of **passive homosexual acts [μαλακοὶ]**, nor **men of active homosexual acts [ἀρσενοκοῖται]**."

The exact same kind of euphemisms was used in the 1980s for the homosexual community. As homosexuality of the 1980s had come out into the open, there has been a joint effort to present a new image to that manner of life. The word "homosexual," with its accent on "sex," has been seen

4

disapprovingly. Into prominence instead was the term "gay." The Concise Oxford Dictionary notes that this word, used in this sense, is a euphemism, a mild word substituted for a harsh or direct one. The same can be said of "homophilia" and "homophile," as sometimes used.

Brief History of the Term Homosexual

The term *Homosexual* was coined in Germany in 1869. It was not used outside of German psychiatrists and psychologists until we got into the 20th century. The first known use of the term homosexual in English is in Charles Gilbert Chaddock's 1892 translation of Richard von Krafft-Ebing's *Psychopathia Sexualis*, a study on sexual practices. The term was popularized by the 1906 Harden–Eulenburg Affair. The word *homosexual* itself had different connotations 100 years ago than today. Although some early writers used the adjective *homosexual* to refer to any single-gender context (such as an all-girls school), today, the term implies a sexual aspect. So, when the 1946 Project claims that the term homosexual was not used in the Bible before 1946, this is true because it was not a common word at the time. It had a different meaning in the early days when the 1901 American Standard Version (ASV) was published or the 1881 English Revised Version (ERV). I mean, the ERV had only been around a few years after the word homosexual was coined. Another reason is that we had growing knowledge of Koine (common) Greek (Biblical Greek) from Desiderius Erasmus' Greek Text in 1536 up unto the 1901 American Standard Version. Still, our understanding grew exponentially from 1900 to the middle of the 1950s. There was a discovery of 500,000 Greek papyri written in Koine.

In January 1897, a trial trench (excavation or depression in the ground) was dug, and it only took a few hours before ancient papyrus materials were found. These included letters, contracts, and official documents. The sand had blown over them, covering them, and for nearly 2,000 years, the dry climate had served as a protection for them.

It took only a mere three months to pull out and recover almost two tons of papyri from Oxyrhynchus. They shipped twenty-five large cases back to England. Over the next ten years, these two courageous scholars, Grenfell and Hunt, archaeologist, and papyrologist, returned each winter to grow their collection. They discovered ancient classical writing, royal ordinances, and contracts mixed in with business accounts private letters, some from Christians, shopping lists, and fragments of many New Testament manuscripts. Our understanding of Greek increased more and more rapidly over the next few decades. This is why the 1946 Revised Standard Version could now use the word homosexual because of a better understanding of

Greek. The word was more common by then and understood as two persons of the same sex having ongoing sexual relations. So, the 1946 Movie is misleading their listeners when they claim that "homosexual" was not used in the Bible before 1946. Moreover, the 1971 Revised Standard Version committee simply folded under pressure, as has been the base with the New Revised Standard Version.

They Claim that In 1946, Theology, History, Culture, and Politics Led to a Biblical Mistranslation of Catastrophic Proportions

They write,

This is our quest to uncover the truth.

More than 45,000 churches today still preach that homosexuality is a sin, citing biblical references that condemn "homosexuals." What would change if churches discovered the truth — the word "homosexual" was added to the Bible in 1946 by mistake?

Executive produced by the director of the 2007 award-winning film, *For the Bible Tells Me So*, *1946: The Mistranslation That Shifted a Culture* is a new documentary that investigates how the word "homosexual" was entered into the Bible, how one man tried to stop it, and how a team of researchers recently unearthed evidence that challenges deeply-held beliefs about LGBTQ+ people and their place in God's kingdom.

Backstory

The first time the word "homosexual" appeared in any bible was in the *Revised Standard Version (RSV)* published in February 11, 1946. In the RSV's translation of 1 Corinthians 6:9, the word "homosexual" was used in lieu of the Greek words "malakoi" and "arsenokoitai." Researchers agree today these words translate loosely to "effeminacy," and "pervert," or "sexual pervert." The decision to use the word "homosexual" instead of the accurate translations was voted on by the RSV committee. *1946* explores how this mistranslation ignited the anti-gay movement within American conservative Christians.

RESPONSE: We already covered this. The word "homosexual" was not used in English until 1892, and the meaning was not the same that we have today. Because of discovering 500,000 koine papyri in the dry sands of Egypt, our understanding of Greek rapidly increased from 1900 to 1946. The

6

only literal translations before the 1946 RSV were the 1881 ERV and the 1901 ASV.

Evidence

Kathy Baldock and Ed Oxford have dedicated their lives to researching the roots of anti-gay theology. As part of their extensive research, they uncovered 90 boxes of notes from the archives at Yale University. Filed in these boxes for over five decades, was a letter sent to the RSV translation committee, written by a young seminarian named David S.

In the letter, David points out the dangerous implications that could come with the mistranslation and misuse of the word "homosexual." Dr. Luther Weigle, the head of the translation committee, wrote a letter back to David S. to acknowledge their mistake and commit to correcting their grave error.

Unfortunately, the revised version of the RSV which replaced "homosexual" with "sexual perverts" wasn't published until 1971 — 25 years after the mistranslation occurred. By then, other translations of the Bible had applied the RSV's use of "homosexual" in biblical texts.

RESPONSE: We should note that Bible scholarship has taken the same path as our secular society over the past 150 years, especially so from 1950 to 2021. The liberal-moderate scholarship is about 80% of all scholarships today. They are constantly seeking to please our society that has grown more and more liberal-progressive each decade.

Effect

Today, the misuse of the word "homosexual" appears in most translations of the Bible, namely in *1 Corinthians 6:9* and *1 Timothy 1:10*. Sadly, this has become the foundation for much of the anti-gay culture that exists today, especially in religious spaces. Many conservative religious leaders have used these biblical texts to condemn and marginalize LGBTQ+ Christians. And society at large has been shaped — at least in part — to believe the idea that sexual and gender minorities must choose between their faith and their identity. We hope the evidence and stories in this film will not only challenge our assumptions, but change our hearts.

From the Director of 1946, "As a lesbian Christian, I have been navigating a religious environment that views me as 'other,' 'less than,' and 'not equal,' for too long."

These beliefs, held by many dear to my heart, have cast a dark, dangerous shadow over my life. After years of searching for my voice, and calling, as a storyteller, my path has led me here. It is my goal to change the Christian narrative and liberate the many LGBTQIA+ people living in the dark; oppressed by bad theology. I want us all to live and be acknowledged as equals, under God's love. There are truths that must be shared. We are here to share those truths." — Sharon "Rocky" Roggio

The Truth about 1 Corinthians 6:9

1 Corinthians 6:9 Updated American Standard Version (UASV) [9] Or do you not know that the unrighteous will not inherit the kingdom of God? Do not be deceived; neither fornicators, nor idolaters, nor adulterers, nor men of passive homosexual acts, nor men of active homosexual acts,[2]

The two Greek terms (μαλακοὶ ... ἀρσενοκοῖται) refer to passive men partners and active men partners in consensual homosexual acts.

Literal Greek: μαλακοὶ soft [men] **οὔτε** nor **ἀρσενοκοῖται** liers with males or male bed partners

Greek Terms

- **μαλακός malakos**; a prim. word; soft, effeminate:—effeminate, soft

- **ἀρσενοκοίτης arsenokoitēs**; sodomite; homosexuals

Lexical Sources

- μαλακός (malakos), ἡ (ē), όν (on): adj.; ≡ Str 3120 2. LN 88.281 homosexual, passive partner in male-to-male sex act.[3]

- μαλακός, ἡ, όν pert. to being passive in a same-sex relationship, effeminate[4]

---

[2] The two Greek terms refer to passive men partners and active men partners in consensual homosexual acts.

[3] James Swanson, Dictionary of Biblical Languages with Semantic Domains: Greek (New Testament) (Oak Harbor: Logos Research Systems, Inc., 1997).

[4] William Arndt et al., A Greek-English Lexicon of the New Testament and Other Early Christian Literature (Chicago: University of Chicago Press, 2000), 613.

- ἀρσενοκοίτης (arsenokoitēs), ου (ou), ὁ (ho): n.masc.; ≡ Str 733— LN 88.280 male homosexual, one who takes the active male role in homosexual intercourse (1Co 6:9),[5]

- ἀρσενοκοίτης, ου, ὁ a male who engages in sexual activity w. a pers. of his own sex, pederast 1 Cor 6:9[6]

These are the passive and active partners in consensual homosexual acts at 1 Corinthians 6:9. God condemns the practice of homosexuality at 1 Timothy 1:10 and the condemnation and prohibition of homosexuality in New Testament times by referring to the historical example of Sodom and Gomorrah at Jude 7.

First Century Bible Background of Homosexuality

Clinton E. Arnold, 1 Corinthians 6:9

Paul uses specialized terminology here.[7] Roman law, in particular the *lex Scantinia* of the mid-second century B.C., legislated about homosexual behavior.[8] Such laws protected Roman citizens against homosexual acts. Corinth as a Roman colony would thus consider homosexual acts with fellow citizens as illegal, but not with noncitizens (i.e., non-Romans) and slaves.

Male prostitutes (6:9). This expression translates *malakoi*. The Greek word *malakos* transferred to the Latin *malacus*. It means in effect "a soft person" and took on the meaning of somebody effeminate. The fact that Latin has no indigenous word for such a person may suggest that a passive participant in a homosexual relationship was not condemned by Roman law so long as he was not a Roman citizen.

Homosexual offenders (6:9). This expression translates the Greek word *arsenokoitai*. This may be a word derived from the LXX [Septuagint] of Leviticus 18:22: "Do not lie with a man as one lies with a woman; that

---

[5] James Swanson, *Dictionary of Biblical Languages with Semantic Domains: Greek (New Testament)* (Oak Harbor: Logos Research Systems, Inc., 1997).

[6] William Arndt et al., *A Greek-English Lexicon of the New Testament and Other Early Christian Literature* (Chicago: University of Chicago Press, 2000), 135.

[7] B. W. Winter, "Homosexual Terminology in 1 Corinthians 6:9: The Roman Context and the Greek Loan-word," in A. N. S. Lane (ed.), *Interpreting the Bible: Historical and Theological Studies in Honor of David F. Wright* (Leicester, U.K.: Apollos, 1997), 275–90 (ch. 14).

[8] This law was passed by the tribune Scantinius c. 146 b.c. See S. Lilja, *Homosexuality in Republican and Augustan Rome* (Helsinki: Societas Scientiarum Fennica, 1982), 112–21.

is detestable." The *malakos* (see previous comment) is probably the passive participant, whereas the *arsenokoitēs* is the active participant. Thus, both stand criticized by Paul within the Christian community. Note, however, that these are but two areas of life that Paul highlights, and the church has not always had the right balance.[9]

David E. Garland, 1 Corinthians 6:9

Pederasty [i.e., man who has sex with boy] was the most common male homosexual act in the ancient world (Schrage 1991: 432). That is because sexual propriety was judged according to social values: "The ancients did not classify kinds of sexual desire or behavior according to the sameness or difference of the sexes of the persons who engaged in a sexual act; rather, they evaluated sexual acts according to the degree to which such acts either violated or conformed to the norms of conduct deemed appropriate to individual sexual actors by reason of their gender, age, and social status" (Halperin, *OCD* 720; cf. Dover 1978: 277). A person's rank and status determined what was considered acceptable or unacceptable. On one side were free males; on the other side were women and slaves. A free male was free to choose women, men, or boys as sexual objects without the majority taking offense as long as he did not demean his status as a free male. A free male could not "indulge in passive acts of love like a woman or a slave" without incurring a stigma (Stegemann 1993: 164). But he could use boys, slaves, or persons of no account with impunity as long as he remained "on top." "Phallic insertion functioned as a marker of male precedence; it also expressed social domination and seniority.... . Any sexual relation that involved the penetration of a social inferior (whether inferior in age, gender, or status) qualified as sexually normal for a male, irrespective of the penetrated person's anatomical sex, whereas to *be* sexually penetrated was always potentially shaming, especially for a free male of citizen status [e.g., Tacitus, *Annales* 11.36]" (Halperin, *OCD* 721). Homosexual acts between free males were regarded with contempt because one partner would have to take on the passive role (insertivity) suited only to women and slaves (Veyne 1987: 204). We see this cultural attitude manifested in Petronius's novel, *Satyricon* (91–100). Two close friends, Encolpius and Ascyltus, fight over the sexual favors of their slave boy, Giton; but they never engage in any homosexual act between themselves.

---

[9] Clinton E. Arnold, *Zondervan Illustrated Bible Backgrounds Commentary: Romans to Philemon.*, vol. 3 (Grand Rapids, MI: Zondervan, 2002), 132–133.

OCD Oxford Classical Dictionary, edited by S. Hornblower and A. Spawforth, 3d ed. (Oxford: Oxford University Press, 1996)

It should be noted also that "neither sexual desire nor sexual pleasure represented an acceptable motive for a boy's compliance with the sexual demands of his lover" (Halperin, *OCD* 721). The younger partner was not to be motivated by, or express, passionate sexual desire for his senior lover, lest he compromise his own future status as a man. As a result, sexually receptive or effeminate males were ridiculed. Society would have considered same-sex sexual acts between two men of equal standing to be shameful. What some in modern society find acceptable—male same-sex eroticism between equals in a committed relationship—would have been condemned in ancient society. Dover (1978: 104) contends that penetration was not regarded as an expression of love but "as an aggressive act demonstrating the superiority of the active to the passive partner." J. Davidson (1997: 169–82) challenges this interpretation as anachronistic but imposes his own biases on the evidence and does not win the argument. Paul differed from his society's sexual mores in condemning all same-sex sexual acts.[10]

Simon J. Kistemaker and William Hendriksen

The next three categories are adulterers, homosexuals, and sodomites. The first Greek expression, *moichoi* (adulterers), describes the sexual sin which a married person commits with someone who either is or is not married; it results in breaking the marriage bond. The next Greek word, *malakoi* (homosexuals), relates to "men and boys who allow themselves to be misused homosexually." This word connotes passivity and submission. By contrast, the third Greek term, *arsenokoitai* (sodomites), represents men who initiate homosexual practices (1 Tim. 1:10). They are the active partners in these pursuits. From Greek and Latin prose, pottery, and sculpture, we learn that preoccupation with sexual practices was prevalent among men in the first century. These men wallowed in homosexual sins and rivaled even the inhabitants of ancient Sodom (Gen. 19:1–10; see also Lev. 18:22; 20:13).[11]

Below we will investigate Romans 1:26-27; 1 Corinthians 6:9; and 1 Timothy 1:10. We have already covered Jude 7 above, so it will not be necessary to go over that material again. We will quote some top New Testament scholars extensively.

---

[10] David E. Garland, *1 Corinthians*, Baker Exegetical Commentary on the New Testament (Grand Rapids, MI: Baker Academic, 2003), 217–218.

[11] Simon J. Kistemaker and William Hendriksen, *Exposition of the First Epistle to the Corinthians*, vol. 18, New Testament Commentary (Grand Rapids: Baker Book House, 1953–2001), 188–189.

Ungodly People Inexcusable

Romans 1:24-32 Updated American Standard Version (UASV)

²⁴ Therefore God gave them over in the lusts of their hearts to impurity, so that their bodies would be dishonored among them. ²⁵ For they exchanged the truth of God for the lie and worshiped and served the creature rather than the Creator, who is blessed forever.¹² Amen.

²⁶ For this reason God gave them over to degrading passions; for their women exchanged natural relations¹³ for those that are contrary to nature, ²⁷ and the men likewise gave up natural relations with women and were violently inflamed in their lust toward one another, males with males committing the shameless deed, and receiving in themselves the due penalty for their error.

²⁸ And just as they did not see fit to acknowledge God any longer, God gave them over to a depraved mind, to do those things which are not proper, ²⁹ being filled with all unrighteousness, wickedness, greed, evil; full of envy, murder, strife, deceit, malice; they are gossips, ³⁰ slanderers, haters of God, insolent, arrogant, boastful, inventors of evil, disobedient to parents, ³¹ without understanding, untrustworthy, unloving, unmerciful; ³² and although they know the ordinance of God, that those who practice such things are worthy of death, they not only do the same, but also give wholehearted approval to those who practice them.

> Wordplays in this text communicate that human sin is rooted in a rejection of the glory of God (Klostermann 1933: 6; Jeremias 1954: 119; Hooker 1966–67: 182). Human beings failed to glorify God (οὐκ ἐδόξασαν, *ouk edoxasan*, v. 21) and exchanged his glory (ἤλλαξαν δόξαν, *ēllaxan doxan*, v. 23) for idolatry. Because people did not honor God by glorifying him, he gave their bodies over to be "dishonored" (ἀτιμάζεσθαι, *atimazesthai*, v. 24), and they had "dishonorable passions" (πάθη ἀτιμίας, *pathē atimias*, v. 26). The parallels in 1 Cor. 11:14–15, 15:43, and 2 Cor. 6:8 indicate that ἀτιμία (*atimia*, dishonor) is contrasted with δόξα (*doxa*, glory; cf. Hooker 1966–67: 182). The disgrace that has invaded human sexual relations is a consequence of rejecting God. The same connection is forged with another word linkage. Those who "exchanged" (ἤλλαξαν, *ēllaxan*, v. 23) God's glory and "exchanged" (μετήλλαξαν, *metēllaxan*, v. 25) his truth "exchanged" (μετήλλαξαν, v. 26) natural sexual relations for that which is

---

¹² Lit *into the ages*

¹³ Or *natural sexual relations*; Lit *natural use*

unnatural. Once again, sexual immorality is evidently a consequence of human idolatry. Finally, those who did not see fit (οὐκ ἐδοκίμασαν, *ouk edokimasan*) to keep God in their knowledge have been handed over to an unfit mind (ἀδόκιμον νοῦν, *adokimon noun*, v. 28). An unfit mind is the fruit of seeing God as unfit. Paul is not referring to Adam in these verses, but he is saying that human beings have gone the way of Adam, and that they have lost glory in trying to retain it.

Some interpreters have understood God's wrath as impersonal and described it in terms of cause and effect.[14] They appeal to the handing over (παρέδωκεν, vv. 24, 26, 28) to sin as evidence that God is not personally angry but merely allows sinners to experience the full consequences of sin. This interpretation betrays the influence of Deism[15] and an Enlightenment worldview rather than explaining Paul's worldview. The OT and Jewish view was that God was vitally and personally involved in his creation. In the OT the judgments inflicted on pagan nations and Israel are invariably the outworking of God's personal decisions. So too here, the handing over to sin is not to be construed impersonally. Three times (vv. 24, 26, 28) it is repeated that "God" (θεός, *theos*) handed over people to sin. To think of "laws" operating impersonally apart from God's personal superintendence reveals that many modern people think differently about his involvement with the created world than the ancient Jews did. The consequences that are inflicted because of sin are the result of God's personal decision. The wrath of God, then, is to be understood in personal terms. God's wrath is not, however, the arbitrary and capricious anger that was so characteristic of the Greek gods. It is his holy and righteous response to those who do not worship and esteem him as God.

Sexual sin is the first consequence of being handed over that Paul mentions (vv. 24, 26–27). Romans 1:24 speaks of being handed over "to uncleanness" (εἰς ἀκαθαρσίαν, *eis akatharsian*). Paul often uses ἀκαθαρσία (2 Cor. 12:21; Gal. 5:19; Eph. 5:3; Col. 3:5; 1 Thess. 4:7) to refer to sexual sin. Paul is perhaps simply describing sexual sin in general terms in verse 24, although his more specific words in verses 26–27 suggest that homosexual relations may be in his mind in verse 24 as well. Why does Paul focus on homosexual relations, especially since it receives little attention elsewhere in his writings (1 Cor. 6:9; 1 Tim. 1:10)? Probably

---

[14] So C. Dodd 1932: 21–24; Hanson 1957: 69, 85; MacGregor 1960–61: 103–6; Byrne 1996: 68; Mounce (1995: 36) rightly critiques this view. Cf. Calvin (1960: 30), who incorrectly concludes that there is no emotion in God. This judgment implies that emotion is a sign of weakness.

[15] Andrews Note: Deism is belief in God based on reason rather than revelation and involving the view, which God has set the universe in motion but does not interfere with how it runs.

13

because it functions as the best illustration of that which is unnatural in the sexual sphere. Idolatry is "unnatural" in the sense that it is contrary to God's intention for human beings. To worship corruptible animals and human beings instead of the incorruptible God is to turn the created order upside down.[16] In the sexual sphere the mirror image of this "unnatural" choice of idolatry is homosexuality (cf. Schlatter 1995: 43; Hays 1986: 191). Human beings were intended to have sexual relations with those of the opposite sex. Just as idolatry is a violation and perversion of what God intended, so too homosexual relations are contrary to what God planned when he created man and woman.

Although verse 26 is ambiguous regarding the precise sense in which women acted contrary to nature, verse 27 clarifies that what is unnatural is same-sex relations.[17] That homosexual relations are contrary to nature, in the sense that they violate what God intended, is communicated in saying that women abandoned "the natural use for that which is contrary to nature" (τὴν φυσικὴν χρῆσιν εἰς τὴν παρὰ φύσιν, *tēn physikēn chrēsin eis tēn para physin*, v. 26), and in saying that men "have left the natural use of women" (ἀφέντες τὴν φυσικὴν χρῆσιν τῆς θηλείας, *aphentes tēn physikēn chrēsin tēs thēleias*, v. 27). The word χρῆσις is often used of sexual relations in Greek writings (BAGD[18] 886), while the word φύσις refers in this context to what God intended in creating men and women (Koester, *TDNT*[19] 9:273; Hays 1986: 196–99; cf. De Young 1988). The word φύσις does not invariably refer to the divine intention in Paul (cf. Rom. 2:14, 27; 11:21, 24 [3 times]; Gal. 2:15; 4:8; Eph. 2:3).[20] At least two pieces of evidence, however, indicate that an argument from the created order is constructed in Rom.

---

[16] After writing this sentence I came upon this observation from Chrysostom (*Homilies on Romans* 4 [on Rom. 1:26–27]), "But when God hath left one, then all things are turned upside down."

[17] Miller (1996) argues that verse 26 refers to unnatural heterosexual practices, not homosexuality. The close parallel with verse 27 renders this claim unlikely. Moreover, the restriction of the criticism to women in verse 26 would be strange since men and women together (according to Miller) were guilty of unnatural sexual behavior. Why would Paul indict only the women if men and women conspired to commit sexual sin? Miller's creative reading should be rejected because it suggests a much more difficult reading that would be less accessible to the Romans than the view that homosexuality is censured in both verses. Some commentators have attempted to explain why women are discussed before men, but no significance should be read from the order.

[18] BAGD *A Greek-English Lexicon of the New Testament and Other Early Christian Literature,* by W. Bauer, W. F. Arndt, F. W. Gingrich, and F. W. Danker, 2d ed. (Chicago: University of Chicago Press, 1979)

[19] *TDNT Theological Dictionary of the New Testament,* edited by G. Kittel and G. Friedrich; translated and edited by G. W. Bromiley, 10 vols. (Grand Rapids: Eerdmans, 1964–76)

[20] The use in 1 Cor. 11:14 is in the midst of a difficult passage. Paul's intention in this text is likely to preserve created distinctions between men and women as well (Fee 1987: 491–530; Schreiner 1991a: 137).

1:26–27. First, Paul selected the unusual words θῆλυς (*thēlys*, female) and ἄρσην (*arsēn*, male) rather than γύνη (*gynē*, woman) and ἀνήρ (*anēr*, man), respectively. In doing so, he drew on the creation account of Genesis, which uses the same words (Gen. 1:27 LXX [Septuagint]; cf. Matt. 19:4; Mark 10:6). These words emphasize the sexual distinctiveness of male and female (Moo 1991: 109), suggesting that sexual relations with the same sex violate the distinctions that God intended in the creation of man and woman. Second, the phrase "contrary to nature" (παρὰ φύσιν) is rooted in Stoic and Hellenistic Jewish traditions that saw homosexual relations as violations of the created order (see below). The latter point is borne out by verse 27, which specifies in three ways what constitutes the unnatural activity for men: (1) in forsaking sexual relations with women (ἀφέντες τὴν φυσικὴν χρῆσιν τῆς θηλείας); (2) in burning in desire for other men (ἐξεκαύθησαν ἐν τῇ ὀρέξει αὐτῶν εἰς ἀλλήλους, *exekauthēsan en tē orexei autōn eis allēlous*); and (3) in doing that which was shameful with other men (ἄρσενες ἐν ἄρσεσιν τὴν ἀσχημοσύνην κατεργαζόμενοι, *arsenes en arsesin tēn aschēmosynēn katergazomenoi*).[21] Verse 27 gives no indication that only specific kinds of homosexual activity are prohibited. Instead, homosexual relations in general are indicted.

Modern controversy over homosexuality has led to a reevaluation of this text. Some scholars argue that Paul does not condemn all forms of homosexuality, but only homosexual acts practiced by people who are "naturally" heterosexual (e.g., Boswell 1980: 109–12). According to this interpretation, to act contrary to nature involves engaging in sexual activity that is contrary to the personal nature or character of the individual. Thus, Paul should not be understood as implying that all homosexuality is contrary to what God intended from creation. He speaks only against homosexual acts that are practiced by those who are heterosexuals by nature.[22]

This interpretation should be rejected since there is no evidence that Paul understood the "nature" of human beings in the individualized and psychological sense that is familiar to us in the twentieth century. Instead,

---

[21] D. Martin (1995: 339–49) argues that Paul indicts homosexuality not because it is contrary to nature but because in Paul's mind homosexual sexuality involves "inordinate desire," just as, say, gluttony is the inordinate desire for food. Martin understands Paul to say that desire for same-sex relations is not contrary to nature; it is proscribed because it is inordinate or beyond nature. Martin does not provide, however, a detailed argument supporting his view of "nature." I am still persuaded (as argued in the exegesis and exposition) that Paul appeals to the created order to justify his proscription. For Paul the very desire for homosexual relations is inordinate and beyond nature.

[22] Countryman (1988: 110–17) argues that Paul does not classify homosexual acts as "sinful" but as impure and unclean. This interpretation has been decisively countered by T. Schmidt (1995: 64–85), whose entire discussion is extraordinarily useful.

in accord with Stoic and Hellenistic Jewish tradition, Paul rejects homosexuality as contrary to the created order—homosexual activity is a violation of what God intended when he created men and women (Hays 1986: 192–94; Malick 1993: 335).[23] Paul's prohibition of all homosexual relations is also supported by the unanimous rejection of homosexuality in Jewish sources (see De Young 1990). For instance, Josephus (*Ag. Ap.* [Against Apion] 2.24 §199) declares that the marriage of a man and woman is "according to nature" (κατὰ φύσιν, *kata physin*), and proceeds to say that the OT law demands the death penalty for intercourse between males. Both Philo (*Spec Laws* [Laws On the Special Laws] 3.7 §38; cf. *Abr.* [On Abraham] 26 §§133–36) and Josephus (*Ag. Ap.* 2.37 §273) specifically criticize homosexual relations as παρὰ φύσιν. The author of the Testament of Naphtali (3.3–4) sees homosexuality as a departure "from the order of nature," and his appeal to creation in verse 3 reveals that he understands this in term of God's created intention.

Scroggs (1983: 109–18) attempts to minimize Paul's negative remarks on homosexuality in Rom. 1:26–27 by arguing that he is simply drawing on Hellenistic Jewish tradition, that probably only pederasty [i.e., man who has sex with boy] is being condemned, and that the focus of the section is theological rather than ethical. The first point reveals the weakness of Scroggs's case. There is no evidence that Paul reverses the unanimous Jewish conviction that homosexuality was sinful (e.g., Gen. 19:1–28; Lev. 18:22; 20:13; Deut. 23:17–18; Wis. 14:26; T. Levi 17.11;[24] Sib. Or. 3.596–600; see also the above citations of Josephus and Philo; and Boughton 1992).[25] Paul's negative comments on homosexuality, even if they are traditional, signal his acceptance of the tradition. The claim that only an abusive form of homosexuality is prohibited, such as pederasty, suffers from lack of evidence. The wording of Rom. 1:26–27 is not restricted to a specific kind of homosexuality but is a general proscription [i.e., banning or prohibition] of the activity. In fact, no mention is made of homosexual relations between men and boys but of "males with males" (ἄρσενες ἐν ἄρσεσιν, *arsenes en arsesin*, v. 27). Moreover, the idea that pederasty is in view is contradicted by the reference to the homosexual acts of women in verse 26 (Malick 1993: 339; Byrne 1996: 76), for pederasty, by definition, involves men and boys, and evidence is lacking that women engaged in

---

[23] So also T. Schmidt 1995; Soards 1995. In surveying the evidence Scroggs demonstrates that in Judaism homosexuality is consistently rejected (1983: 66–84), while in the Greco-Roman world (1983: 17–65) there was significant acceptance of homosexuality.

[24] Levi Testament of Levi

[25] In fact, Scroggs himself (1983:66–84) demonstrates that the Jews of Paul's day were distinct from Greeks in that they consistently rejected homosexuality.

16

sexual activity with girls. Finally, Scroggs artificially separates theology from ethics in Pauline thought, implying that the vices listed would not be part of Paul's ethical exhortations. But theology and ethics are closely wedded in all of Paul's letters. Any attempt to drive a wedge between them is unsatisfactory. The rejection of God theologically is concretely illustrated in evil that is promulgated by human beings.

Sheppard (1985) admits that Paul's rejection of homosexuality cannot be explained away but argues that loving homosexual relations can be accepted in the light of the canon as a whole and the recognition that our understanding of the Word of God advances as we gain more knowledge about homosexuality. To say that the whole of Scripture supports homosexuality is weak, since there is no canonical acceptance of homosexuality. Sheppard's argument depends ultimately not on the canon, but on his conviction that recent study and human experience validate homosexuality as a legitimate lifestyle. Furnish (1985: 79–80; so also M. Davies 1995) is more straightforward in saying that we can no longer accept Paul's view on homosexuality, for he was limited in his understanding of it.[26] For those who accept the Pauline proscription as authoritative (as I do), avoidance of homosexual relations is the path of happiness and holiness.

The last clause in verse 27 has engendered some controversy. What is the "penalty" (ἀντιμισθίαν, *antimisthian*) that people receive in themselves? The context suggests that the "penalty" is not something in addition to homosexuality. The penalty is rather being handed over to the sin of homosexuality itself. The words ἣν ἔδει τῆς πλάνης αὐτῶν (*hēn edei tēs planēs autōn*, which was necessary of their error) point in this direction. The πλάνη here is not an inadvertent mistake but the rejection of the true God for idols (Byrne 1996: 77). Thus people had to be (ἔδει) handed over to punishment precisely because they had scorned God's glory. Once again, the main theme of the text is driven home. The foundational sin of refusing to thank and glorify God leads to other sins.

The connection between rejecting God and human sin is forged again with the vice list appearing in verses 29–31. Vice lists are common in Paul (1 Cor. 5:10–11; 6:9–10; 2 Cor. 12:20; Gal. 5:19–21; Eph. 4:31; 5:3–5; Col. 3:5, 8; 1 Tim. 1:9–10; 6:4–5; 2 Tim. 3:2–4; Titus 3:3), and some of the vices are occasionally included because of problems in the church addressed. The list here, though, does not reflect ethical problems in the church in Rome. The list is a general and wide-ranging depiction of human sin. In

---

[26] For helpful surveys of the issue along with practical ministry suggestions see T. Schmidt 1995; J. Taylor 1995.

introducing the vices Paul uses Stoic terminology (ποιεῖν τὰ μὴ καθήκοντα, *poiein ta mē kathēkonta*, to do things that are not fitting, v. 28). To conclude that Paul is charging every single Gentile of these specific sins (Räisänen 1983: 98) is unnecessary. Instead, he enunciates the principle that all Gentiles commit sin, in thought, word, and deed (see Laato 1991: 113–15).

The vice list is organized into three main parts. First, the participle πεπληρωμένους (*peplērōmenous*, being filled) introduces four words that all conclude with -ια (*-ia*). These words are all general descriptions of human sin: ἀδικίᾳ (*adikia*, unrighteousness), πονηρίᾳ (*ponēria*, wickedness), πλεονεξίᾳ (*pleonexia*, covetousness), and κακίᾳ (*kakia*, wickedness or malice). Precise distinctions should not be drawn among the various words; they are used for effect to denote in a comprehensive way the wickedness of human beings. Second, five words modify μεστούς (*mestous*, full): φθόνου (*phthonou*, envy), φόνου (*phonou*, murder), ἔριδος (*eridos*, strife), δόλου (*dolou*, deceit), and κακοηθείας (*kakoētheias*, malice). Assonance is present in the first two words. It is unlikely that Paul is being so specific as to indicate that the last four sins listed stem from envy (Cranfield 1975: 130). Murder, strife, deceit, and ill will too often exist where envy is not present, and thus more conclusive evidence would be needed to establish such a connection. Finally, twelve words or phrases all in the accusative, appositional to αὐτούς (*autous*, them) in verse 28, conclude the list. The first two sins describe those who destroy others' reputations (ψιθυριστάς, *psithyristas*, gossips; καταλάλους, *katalalous*, slanderers), and once again we should not be overly specific in distinguishing these from one another. The next six expressions seem to be allied in terms of the shocking depth of evil. Θεοστυγεῖς (*theostygeis*, haters of God) could possibly be translated as "hated by God" (so Schlatter 1995: 44), but since the rest of the words in this list refer to human evil, the translation "haters of God" is preferable (Calvin 1960: 38). The words ὑβριστάς (*hybristas*, insolent), ὑπερηφάνους (*hyperēphanous*, arrogant), and ἀλαζόνας (*alazonas*, braggarts) are thematically related insofar as they point to the self-importance and rudeness of those who are convinced of their superiority. The next two vices are linked in that they are both two-word phrases: ἐφευρετὰς κακῶν (*epheuretas kakōn*, inventors of evil) and γονεῦσιν ἀπειθεῖς (*goneusin apeitheis*, disobedient to parents). Both signify the depth of evil. The former highlights their creativity in performing evil, while the latter reveals that sin ruptures relationships in the home. The list concludes with some rhetorical force by four terms that are joined together: ἀσυνέτους (*asynetous*, foolish), ἀσυνθέτους (*asynthetous*, treacherous), ἀστόργους (*astorgous*, without natural affection), and ἀνελεήμονας (*aneleēmonas*, without mercy). All four words begin with ἀ-, and assonance connects the first two. The first three words all end with -ους, while the -ας ending on the last word is closely similar in sound. Dunn (1988a: 53) nicely catches the sense and partially reproduces the effect in translating the four terms "senseless, faithless, loveless, merciless," which I have adopted in my translation.

The depth and full weight of human sin is communicated with verse 32, which concludes this section. Flückiger (1954: 156–57) argues that verse 32 is not the conclusion of Paul's indictment of the Gentiles but is addressed to the Jews. This interpretation should be rejected since οἵτινες (*hoitines*, who) and the reference to the sins just described in the previous verses show a close connection between verse 32 and what precedes. The διὸ (*dio*, therefore) commencing 2:1 suggests that the chapter break between the two sections in our Bibles is appropriate.

The people in view are those who practice the evil described in the previous verses (αὐτὰ ποιοῦσιν, *auta poiousin*, they do them; οἱ τὰ τοιαῦτα πράσσοντες, *hoi ta toiauta prassontes*, those who practice such things). The things (αὐτά, τοιαῦτα) they practice probably include all the vices listed in 1:24–31. It is remarkable, despite their rejection of the true God and the darkening of their understanding (vv. 21–23), that they are still keenly aware of God's disapproval of their behavior. In fact, their awareness is even greater than this. They know "the ordinance of God" (τὸ δικαίωμα τοῦ θεοῦ, *to dikaiōma tou theou*), which is specified in the subsequent ὅτι (*hoti*, that) clause. God's ordinance is that those who indulge in such behavior are "worthy of death" (ἄξιοι θανάτου, *axioi thanatou*). It follows, then, that Gentiles, without specifically having the Mosaic law, are aware of the moral requirements contained in that law (cf. Thielman 1994a: 169; Wilckens 1978: 115). They not only know that God disapproves of their behavior but they also know that it deserves the punishment of death (cf. 6:23). Nonetheless, they continue to engage in such wicked behavior.

The depth of their evil is even greater. This is indicated by the οὐ μόνον ... ἀλλὰ καί (*ou monon ... alla kai*, not only ... but also) structure of the text. Not only do they continue to practice evil that they know deserves God's sentence of death, but they also "give commendation to those who practice these things" (συνευδοκοῦσιν τοῖς πράσσουσιν, *syneudokousin tois prassousin*). This verse manifests considerable diversity in the textual witnesses, presumably because many scribes (like many modern interpreters) questioned how encouraging others to practice evil was a graver evil than actually doing the evil (see the additional note on 1:32). But Cranfield (1975: 133–35) is right in arguing that the text is saying just what it appears to say. He notes correctly that the person who commits evil, even though his or her actions are inexcusable, can at least plead the mitigating circumstances of the passion of the moment. Those who encourage others to practice evil do so from a settled and impassioned conviction. Cranfield (1975: 135) says: "But there is also the fact that those who condone and applaud the vicious actions of others are actually making a deliberate contribution to the setting up of public opinion favourable to vice, and so to the corruption of an indefinite number of other people." The full extent of the rejection of God becomes evident in such an attitude. His judgment is known, yet people are encouraged to pursue evil anyway. Those who encourage others to pursue evil commit a greater evil in that they foment the spread of evil and are complicit in the destruction of others. The hatred of God is so entrenched that people are willing to risk future judgment in order to carry out their evil desires.[27] Once again, the text hints that the fundamental sin that informs all others is a refusal to delight in or submit to God's lordship. God's wrath is rightly inflicted on those who not only practice evil but find their greatest delight in it.[28]

1 Corinthians 6:9 Updated American Standard Version (UASV) [9] Or do you not know that the unrighteous will not inherit the kingdom of God? Do not be deceived; neither fornicators, nor idolaters, nor adulterers, nor men of passive homosexual acts, nor men of active homosexual acts,[29]

1 Timothy 1:10 Updated American Standard Version (UASV)

[10] the sexually immoral ones, men who lie with men,[30] kidnappers, liars, perjurers, and whatever else is contrary to sound teaching,

1 Corinthians 6:9 and 1 Timothy 1:10

Paul also speaks against homosexuality in 1 Corinthians 6:9 and 1 Timothy 1:10. In both texts he used the term *arsenokoitai* [male partner in homosexual intercourse] to designate the sin of homosexuality. Paul's use of the term represents its first occurrence in Greek literature. David Wright is likely correct in suggesting that Paul derived the term from Leviticus 18:22 and 20:13.[31] When we look at both of these texts in the

---

[27] Calvin (1960: 38) remarks, "A man who feels shame may still be healed; but when such a lack of shame has been acquired through the practice of sin, that vice, and not virtue, pleases us and has our approval, there is no more any hope of amendment."

[28] Thomas R. Schreiner, *Romans*, vol. 6, Baker Exegetical Commentary on the New Testament (Grand Rapids, MI: Baker Books, 1998), 92–100.

[29] The two Greek terms refer to passive men partners and active men partners in consensual homosexual acts

[30] men who are sexually active with members of his own sex.

[31] David F. Wright, 'Homosexuals or Prostitutes? The Meaning of *Arsenokoitai* (1 Cor. 6:9 1 Tim. 1:10)', *Vigiliae Christianae* 38 (1984): 125–53. Dale B. Martin criticizes the interpretation supported by

LXX, we can see the argument: *kai meta arsenos ou koimēthēse koitēn gynaikos bdelygma gar estin* (Lev. 18:22); *kai hos an koimēthē meta arsenos koitēn gynaikos bdelygma epoiēsan amphoteroi thanatousthōsan enochoi eisin* (Lev. 20:13). What Wright argues, and other scholars have followed him here, is that the Pauline term *arsenokoitai* [male partner in homosexual intercourse] is a Pauline innovation deriving from the phrase, *arsenos koitēn* in the two texts from Leviticus. The term refers, then, to those who bed other males. In other words, it is a vivid way of denoting same sex intercourse between males. The other word used to designate same sex relations in 1 Corinthians 6:9 is *malakoi*. This word refers to the passive partner sexually, an effeminate male who plays the role of a female.

Both 1 Corinthians 6:9 and 1 Timothy 1:10, also proscribe [ban or condemn] homosexuality in general. Dale Martin suggests that the term *arsenokoitai* [male partner in homosexual intercourse] refers to those who exploit others sexually, but cannot be limited to same sex relations.[32] Such a broadening of the term, however, does not fit with either the background of the term in Leviticus 18:22 and 20:13 or the basic meaning of the word: bedding a male. Furthermore, the pairing of *arsenokoitai* with *malakoi* in 1 Corinthians 6:9 indicates that homosexual relations are in view. Paul could have used the more technical term *paiderastēs* (a pederast [man who has sex with boy]) if he had intended to restrict his comments to exploitative sex. Furthermore, if the only problem in view were sex that exploits others, there would be no need for Paul to mention the passive partner as well since he is the one being oppressed, and not the oppressor.

Robin Scroggs suggests another interpretation. He argues that the word *andrapodistais* (slave-dealers) in 1 Timothy 1:10 intimates that *arsenokoitai* refers to the slave dealers who sell boys and girls as slaves for brothel houses.[33] Scroggs's view is scarcely persuasive, it is hard to believe that kidnappers were exclusively involved in the sex-trade business. Moreover, the term for slave-dealers is lacking in the 1 Corinthians 6:9 context, and it can scarcely be imported there to explain the term *arsenokoitai*. Finally, there is no reason to think that the term slave-dealers casts any light on the meaning of *arsenokoitai* in the vice list in 1 Timothy

Wright in '*Arsenokoites* and *Malakos*, Meaning and Consequences', in *Biblical Ethics and Homosexuality: Listening to Scripture*, ed. Robert L. Brawley (Louisville: Westminster John Knox, 1996), 119–23, In turn Gagnon defends Wright's view and exposes the weaknesses in Martin's interpretation (*Homosexual Practice*, 312–36).

[32] Martin, '*Arsenokoites and Malakos*', 119–23

[33] Scroggs, *New Testament and Homosexuality*, 118–21.

1:9–10. The sins listed represent particularly egregious violations of the ten commandments.

Alternative explanations are provided for *malakoi* as well. Scroggs thinks the reference is to effeminate callboys and prostitution.[34] In reply we can say that Paul's indictment would include such activities, but there is insufficient evidence to limit what Paul says here to male prostitution. Dale Martin argues that effeminacy broadly conceived is in view, so that the *malakoi* adorn themselves with soft and expensive clothes, consume gourmet foods, are pre-occupied with their hair-style, wear perfume, engage in heterosexual sex excessively, masturbate, are gluttons, lazy, and cowards, and also accept phallic penetration by another male.[35] Martin thinks such a view is misogynist and should not be endorsed in our day. The Pauline evidence, however, does not verify Martin's view. In 1 Corinthians 6:9 the word *malakoi* is paired with *arsenokoitai*, and the combination of the two terms indicates that same sex relations are in view, not heterosexual sex or effeminate behaviour in general. Paul, of course, in the very same verse says that those who live sexually immoral lives as heterosexuals will be excluded from the kingdom as well, but he does not have such a notion in mind when he uses the terms *arsenokoitai* and *malakoi*.

Sons and Daughters of Adam

As noted earlier, the biblical prohibition on homosexuality is questioned, because we allegedly have knowledge about homosexuality that was not available to biblical writers. For instance, it is sometimes said that homosexuality is genetic, and biblical writers were not cognizant of this truth. It is not my purpose here to delve into the question of the genetic character of homosexuality. The scientific evidence supporting such a conclusion, however, is not compelling. Most studies yield the rather common sense conclusion that homosexuality is the result of both nature and nurture, and cannot be wholly explained by genetic factors.[36]

However, I do want to look at the perspective of the Scriptures, relative to so-called genetic characteristics. Even if some sins could be traced to our genetics, it would not exempt us from responsibility for such sins. The Scriptures teach that all human beings are born into this world as sons and daughters of Adam, and hence they are by nature children of

---

[34] Scroggs, *New Testament and Homosexuality*, 106–109.

[35] Martin, '*Arsenokoites and Malakos*', 124–28.

[36] See, e.g., Stanton L. Jones & Mark A. Yarhouse, *Homosexuality: The Use of Scientific Research in the Church's Moral Debate* (Downers Grove: InterVarsity, 2000); Jeffrey Satinover, *Homosexuality and the Politics of Truth* (Grand Rapids: Baker, 1996); Schmidt. *Straight and Narrow?*, 131–59; Gagnon, *Homosexual Practice*, 396–432.

wrath (Eph. 2:3). They are dead in trespasses in sins (Eph. 2:1, 5), and have no inclination to seek God or to do what is good (Rom. 3:10–11). We come into the world as those who are spiritually dead (Rom. 5:12, 15), so that death reigns over the whole human race (Rom. 5:17). Indeed, human beings are condemned by virtue of Adam's sin (Rom. 5:16, 18). Such a radical view of sin in which we inherit a sinful nature from Adam means that sinful predispositions are part of our personalities from our inception. Hence, even if it were discovered that we are genetically predisposed to certain sinful behaviours like alcoholism or homosexuality, such discoveries would not eliminate our responsibility for our actions, nor would it suggest that such actions are no longer sinful. The Scriptures teach that we are born as sinners in Adam, while at the same time they insist we should not sin and are responsible for the sin we commit. We enter into the world as slaves of sin (Rom. 6:6, 17), but we are still morally blameworthy for capitulating to the sin that serves as our master.

New Persons in Christ

When we think of a NT perspective on homosexuality, we must remember the proclamation of the gospel, the truth that those who are in Christ are new persons. In other words, we have substantial evidence that those who struggle with the sin of homosexuality can live a new life by God's grace. We are enabled to live new lives because of who we are in Christ. Those who put their trust in Christ are justified by faith (Rom. 5:1). They have peace with God and are reconciled to him through the cross of Christ (Rom. 5:1, 10). They are adopted as God's children (Rom. 8:14–17). They are redeemed and liberated from the power of sin, so that they may be zealous for good works (Tit. 2:14). They are now saved by grace through faith (Eph. 2:8). They have been born again through the Holy Spirit.[37] They are a new creation (Gal. 6:16; 2 Cor. 5:17). All people enter the world as sons and daughters of Adam and so are under the dominion of 'the old man'. But now, by virtue of union with Christ, they are clothed with the 'new man'.[38] They have put the old man off and have been endowed with the new man. Those who are in Christ are sanctified (1 Cor. 1:30; 6:11), so that they stand before God as those who are holy and clean in his sight. Their sins are truly forgiven, so that they do not live under the shackles of the past (Eph. 1:14; Col. 2:11–14).

The Continuing Struggle with Sin and the Promise of Moral Perfection

---

[37] John 1:12, 3:3, 5, 8.

[38] Rom. 6:6; Col. 3:9–10; Eph. 2:15; cf. Eph. 4:24.

23

We face two dangers here. We may under-emphasize our newness in Christ, so that the redemption accomplished for us is negated or trivialized. On the other hand, we may fall prey to an over-realized eschatology that underestimates the continuing presence of sin in the lives of believers. The already, but not yet dimension of Christian teaching is immensely practical when it comes to understanding sanctification. First John 3:1–3 makes it clear that believers are not all that we will be. We will be conformed fully to the likeness of Jesus only when he returns. Hence, in the meantime, believers continue to struggle with sin. We stand in the right before God by virtue of the work of Christ, but we are not perfected. The emblem of the continuing presence of sin in our lives is our mortal body. The NT regularly teaches that we will experience moral perfection when our corruptible bodies become incorruptible, when this mortal puts on immortality.[39] In the meantime, we continue the struggle against sin as long as we are in our bodies until the day of resurrection (Phil. 3:20–21). The resurrection of our bodies testifies that the bodies are not inherently sinful, but as sons and daughters of Adam we are born into the world with sin reigning over us as whole persons (Rom 5:12–19).

The tension of Christian experience surfaces here. We are new creations in Christ and liberated from the power of sin, but at the same time, we await the fullness of our redemption. The newness of our redemption in Christ does not mean that we are completely free of sin. Rather, as believers we continue to battle against, and struggle with sin every day. First Peter 2:11 says, 'Beloved, I urge you as sojourners and exiles to abstain from the passions of the flesh, which wage war against your soul.' Notice that the passions and desires from the flesh are still powerful in all believers. They are so strong that they war against us.

We might think that we will not have any desires to do evil as believers in Jesus Christ, but as long as we are in the [imperfect] body, desires for sin, sometimes incredibly powerful desires, will be ours. Such desires do not mean that we are failures, or that we are not truly believers. They are a normal part of the Christian life before the day of resurrection. We ought not to think, therefore, that the newness we have in Christ means that believers will have no desire to return to a homosexual lifestyle. The newness we have in Christ does not mean that we are freed from old temptations. There is a progressive and even sometimes slow growth in holiness in our Christian lives. Indeed, we can sin dramatically as believers, even if we have been Christians for a long time. Even when we sin in such

---

[39] Rom. 8:10–11, 23; 1 Cor. 15:52–54; Eph. 1:14.

a way, there is no excuse for sinning [i.e., living in sin], and we are called to a deep sorrow and repentance for the evil in our lives.

This explains why we must fight the fight of faith afresh every day. Peter does not upbraid his readers for having desires to do wrong, but he does exhort them to abstain from these fleshly desires that war against our souls. In Romans 8:13, the apostle Paul says that believers are to put to death by the Spirit the desires of the body. Again, from this verse we see that Christians still face sin since they live in corruptible bodies, and the battle against sin is so fierce that the deeds of the body must be slain. They must be put to death. This fits with Colossians 3:5 where we are exhorted to put to death our members that are on earth. The metaphor of putting these desires and actions to death demonstrates that we are not talking about something easy and simple here.

The NT, of course, does not simply leave us with the message: 'Just say "no" '. It trumpets the grace of God in Jesus Christ that liberates us from the mastery and tyranny of sin. Those who have died and risen with Christ are no longer slaves to sin (Rom. 6). The power and dominion of sin has been broken decisively, so that we are now free from the tentacles of sin and are enabled to live in a way that pleases God. Romans 8:13 exhorts us to conquer sinful actions by the power of the Holy Spirit. We realize that we cannot triumph over sin in our own strength. We call on the Spirit to help us in our hour of need, and we realize that we will not be full of the Spirit (Eph. 5:18) unless the Word of Christ dwells in us richly (Col. 3:16). We remember the truth of the gospel that we are loved because Christ Jesus died for us. We are adopted, justified, reconciled, redeemed, and holy in Christ. The exhortation to live a new live comes from a Father who has loved us and delivered us from final condemnation. It is from a Father who promises to complete what he has started on the last day (Phil. 1:6). We have the promise that we will be fully, and finally sanctified (1 Thess. 5:23–24). Hence, we trust his promises to strengthen and free us from the allure of sin. We are not yet perfected, but we are changing by his Spirit. And we are changing because we have been changed and will be changed from one degree of glory to another, just as from the Lord who is the Spirit of freedom (2 Cor. 3:17–18).[40]

From what we have above, we can clearly see that there is absolutely no ambiguity in the Bible at all. God designed Adam and Eve to procreate, and sex is between one man and one woman. (Gen. 1:27, 28; Lev 18:22; Pro 5:18-19) Fornication in Scripture is a reference to sexual sin by homosexual and

---

[40] Thomas R. Schreiner, "A New Testament Perspective on Homosexuality," *Themelios* 31, no. 3 (2006): 70–75.

heterosexual conduct. (Gal. 5:19-21) We have certainly overturned many of the arguments given by the LGBT homosexual community in the above. God had warned of those who would twist (distort) the meaning of the Scriptures. Since Jesus does not directly mention homosexuality, but the apostle Paul does so explicitly many times in a condemnatory judgment kind of way, the only recourse for those that favor homosexuality is to undermine Paul's arguments by twisting (distorting) the meaning of the text. The irony is that Peter said this very thing would happen. Peter wrote of Paul, "and regard the patience of our Lord as salvation; just as also our beloved brother Paul, according to the wisdom given him, wrote to you, as also **in all his letters**, speaking in them of these things, in which are **some things hard to understand**, which **the untaught and unstable distort**, as they do also the rest of the Scriptures, to their own destruction." (2 Pet. 3:15-16) We have followed the advice from Peter's first letter. "But in your hearts honor Christ the Lord as holy, **always being prepared to make a defense** to anyone who asks you for a reason for the hope that is in you; yet do it **with gentleness and respect**, having a good conscience, so that, when you are slandered, those who revile your good behavior in Christ may be put to shame." – 1 Peter 3:15-16.

The Bible's Viewpoint of Same-Sex Attraction

However, the Bible does not condone hating those who struggle with same-sex attraction, but we are to hate the sin. However, we are to make a stand against sin that is against the moral code of our Creator, and we are **not** to cave to public opinion. Our Christian lifestyle is reflective of the moral code within Scripture, and we have a right to our position by the Creator himself. There is no reason that we should be ashamed of our viewpoint.

1 Peter 2:17 New Living Translation (NLT)

17 Respect everyone, and love your Christian brothers and sisters. Fear God, and respect the king.

Christians should not have an irrational hatred for those that struggle with same-sex attraction. We are to respect all people. Anyone who is spewing hatred, he is not truly acting Christlike. (Matt. 7:12) We are to reject same-sex relationships, the conduct, not the person. For those who are advocates for gay rights, this is their viewpoint, and we **respectfully** disagree and **respectfully** articulate as to why. Nevertheless, we do not accept persons as being truly Christian or members of a Christian congregation living in any sin, which includes homosexuality. – Revelation 2:5; 1 Corinthians 5:5-13; 1 Timothy 1:19, 20; 3 John 9, 10.

If some argue that Jesus visited sinners and that he was tolerant of others, this is mixing some truth, but also misleading at the same time. Indeed, Jesus spent time with sinners, but he did not ever condone their sin, nor did he ever look favorably upon those who practiced sin, i.e., lived in sin. – Matthew 18:15-17.

Some may make the point I made in the above but take it a step further. They may say, "I am born this way. It is not my fault. Why should I be punished or miss out on love because of inheriting a genetic predisposition?"

We could respond that the Bible does not **directly** address the genetic predisposition of same-sex attraction, but then again, it does not address the mental issues of bipolar either. It is not a science textbook, nor is it a mental health guide. Thus, we should not look for it to resolve the specifics. However, it does address certain thinking and certain actions. Therefore, the Bible might not explicitly address the genetic, but it does address same-sex acts. Why did I say that the genetic predisposition of same-sex attraction was not **directly addressed**? This is because it is **indirectly addressed**. The Bible tells us "just as through one man sin entered into the world, and death through sin, and so death spread to all men, because all sinned." (Rom. 5:12) This one Bible verse encapsulates what happened after God created Adam and Eve. Sin (ἁμαρτία hamartia) means missing the mark of perfection. We are told all throughout the Scriptures just how far off the mark we are. Genesis 6:5 and 8:21 tell us that we are all mentally bent toward evil. Jeremiah 17:9 tells us that our hearts (inner person and thinking) are treacherous, and we cannot even know it. The apostle Paul tells us in the book of Romans that our natural desire is to do evil. So, if the genetic predisposition of same-sex attraction is true, it is a product of our inherited sin like any other disorder or disease.

Some have argued that addictive personalities are genetically predisposed (gambling, drugs, alcohol, intense opposite-sex attraction, and pedophilia), as well as anger and rage are also viewed as genetic. Giving these ones the same benefit of the doubt as to the leanings being genetic, would we approve of a man who beats his wife, or another man who sexually abuses women because they may be predisposed to those desires. Certainly not. We would send him to Christian counseling and expect him to get control over his body and mind by putting on the mind of Christ. Would we excuse a genetically predisposed man as a pedophile who acts on his sexual desire for children? No, we would scream, lock him up and throw away the key. We would acknowledge that the wife-beater and the pedophile struggle with these desires, and we would expect that they would not put themselves in an innocent appearing situation. Moreover, we would expect them through

27

redemptive therapy through biblical counseling to get and maintain control over themselves.

What the Bible offers is reasonable, and it does not condone homophobic mindsets. The Bible expects those who have same-sex attraction to apply the same counsel as those with intense opposite-sex attraction.

1 Corinthians 6:18 Updated American Standard Version (UASV)

[18] **Flee from sexual immorality.*** Every other sin that a man commits is outside the body, but the sexually immoral person sins against his own body.[41]

Hundreds of thousands, if not millions of men and women, suffer from intense sexual attraction and addiction. The Bible expects them to get control over their body, not give into temptation. The same is expected with those with same-sex attraction.

> ***** Paul began his conclusion to this section with an abrupt command: **Flee … immorality**. It is likely that the apostle had in mind Joseph's example of fleeing Potiphar's wife (Gen. 39:12). Paul instructed the young pastor Timothy in a similar way (2 Tim. 2:22). Rather than moderate resistance to immorality, Paul insisted on radical separation.
>
> Paul's radical advice rested on the uniqueness of sexual sin. In contrast with **all other sins**, immorality is **against** one's **own body**. The meaning of these words is difficult to determine. Many sins, such as substance abuse, gluttony, and suicide, have detrimental effects on the body. Paul's words do not refer to disease and/or other damage caused by sin. Instead, his words are linked to the preceding discussion of 6:12–17. There Paul established that Christians' bodies are joined with Christ so that they become "members of Christ" (6:15) himself.
>
> Sexual union with a prostitute violates one's body by bringing it into a wrongful "one flesh" union, and by flaunting the mystical union with Christ (6:15). It is in this sense that sexual immorality is a unique sin against the body. It violates the most significant fact about believers' physical existence: their bodies belong to Christ. – (Pratt Jr 2000, 101)

---

[41] Help is available for all who struggle with same sex attraction and those who struggle with intense opposite-sex attraction. http://www.aacc.net/

Sexual Immorality: (זָנָה zanah; πορνεία porneia) A general term for immoral sexual acts of any kind: such as adultery, prostitution, sexual relations between people not married to each other, homosexuality, and bestiality. – Num. 25:1; Deut. 22:21; Matt. 5:32; 1 Cor. 5:1.

The Bible refers to sexual relations outside of marriage as "fornication." The sound direction is to "flee from sexual immorality," for no "sexually immoral" person "has any inheritance in the kingdom of the Christ and of God." (1 Cor. 6:18; Eph. 5:5) Also, the Bible says that none who "are guilty either of adultery or of homosexual perversion . . . will possess the kingdom of God." (1 Cor. 6:9-10, New English Bible) Just imagine how much grief and sorrow, hatred and disease could be eradicated by heeding the Bible's advice!—Rom. 1:24-27.

God created man and woman to enjoy sexual relations only within the arrangement of marriage between a male and a female. (Genesis 1:27, 28; Leviticus 18:22; Proverbs 5:18, 19) The Bible denounces sexual relations that are **not** between a husband and wife, regardless of whether it is homosexual or heterosexual behavior. (1 Corinthians 6:18) This includes sexual intercourse, caressing or stroking another person's genitals, and engaging in oral or anal sex.

The Bible's position is not unreasonable. It simply directs those with same-sex attraction urges to do the same thing that is expected of those who have an opposite-sex attraction, to "flee from sexual immorality." (1 Corinthians 6:18) The fact is that millions of heterosexuals face desires and temptations every day of their lives, who want to conform to the Bible's standards. They seek to apply self-control, notwithstanding any temptations they might face daily. Those with same-sex desires can do the same thing if they genuinely want to please God. - Deuteronomy 30:19.

CHAPTER 2 The Bible's Viewpoint of Homosexuality

 We have already covered what the Bible has to say extensively in Chapter 1. So, here this will be a continuation of that. The USA has the only large mainstream church ever to consecrate an openly gay bishop (Gene Robinson), the Episcopal Church in the United States of America. A vast majority voted in an openly gay pastor of the biggest Evangelical Lutheran Church in Saint Paul, MN (Bradley Schmeling), as the senior pastor. The Presbyterian Church (U.S.A.) is now allowing openly gay men and women in same-sex relationships to be ordained as clergy.

The issue is so divisive that it has split a major denomination in half. Those who see somebody who is sexually involved with members of his or her own sex as being just an alternative lifestyle and acceptable as a church member or pastor, while the other side sees it as contrary to nature and not acceptable for a church member, let alone a pastor, or bishop. Both sides use God's Word as a means of saying that their position is biblical. However, the law of noncontradiction helps us appreciate it is impossible for same-sex couples who are actively in a sexual relationship to be both biblical and not biblical. In other words, someone is wrong in his or her interpretation of Scripture.

Some who support the right for church members, pastors, and bishops to be actively involved sexually with a person of the same sex will argue,

I believe God made us all in His image; He did not make a mistake. We love whom we love because God wants us to.

In making this comment, the supporters are thinking of the following text as their support,

Genesis 1:27 Updated American Standard Version (UASV)

27 So God created man in his own image, in the image of God he created him; male and female he created them.

First, it should be noted that Genesis 1:27 informs us of when Adam and Eve were perfect and had not yet rebelled, bringing sin (missing the mark of perfection into the world). God made Adam and Eve perfect but gave them free will to willfully choose to abuse and abuse, they did. Once they were expelled from the Garden, inherited sin was passed on from generation to generation. Of course, the preflood generations all lived close to 1,000 years. To mention a few of the preflood people and their lifespan, we read that all the days that Adam lived were 930 years, all the days of Seth were 912 years, all the days of Methuselah were 969 years. If we consider the progression after the flood, we will notice a dramatic drop in lifespans. Shem, who came through the flood, lived 600 years. (Gen 11:10, 11) Peleg lived 239 years. Abraham was born 352 years after the flood and died at the age of 175. Moses, four generations later, would live to 120 years of age.

After the flood, the lifespans of those who survived the flood to the other side, and postflood people, dropped drastically. This could be because the floodwaters that fell from the heavens had served as a shield in the heavens before their falling, protecting the people from the harmful radiation that would have increased without such protection. In addition, it must be remembered that preflood people were closer to perfect, and this is why they lived longer lives. A prayer of Moses, the man who penned the book of Genesis in the latter part of the sixteenth century B.C.E. under inspiration, spoke of a time, "As for the days of our years, within them are seventy years or if by strength eighty years, and their pride is trouble and disaster, for it passes quickly and we fly away." (Ps. 90:10, LEB) Today, science can actually do genetic screening, DNA analysis for medical purposes: the analysis of DNA samples of a group of people carried out in order to find out whether they carry the genes associated with specific **inherited diseases** or disorders. We have inherited diseases and mental disorders that can even skip generations, which affect us all because we are imperfect, unlike Adam and Eve. "... Sin came into the world through one man, and death through sin, and so death spread to all men because all sinned." – Romans 5:12.

What does the Bible say about Homosexuality? What does it say about same-sex marriage? What does it say about same-sex attraction? Is it a sin to be homosexually active? If it is a sin, then why does homosexuality exist? Is God just being unfair, or is it more complicated than that? Before going on, it might be good to qualify some terms. Many people dealing with same-sex attraction find the word homosexual offensive because it implies one who is sexually active with a person of the same sex. We must admit some struggle with same-sex attraction but realize that the Bible condemns such activity, so they must constantly maintain control over themselves.

Baker *Encyclopedia of Psychology and Counseling* says "'Homosexuality' means 'same or like sexuality' and derives from the Greek word *homoitas* (likeness, similarity, or agreement). Sexuality is the God-given drive in every person toward wholeness and includes emotional, cognitive, psychological, and spiritual dimensions. This drive is expressed in adult human beings

31

emotionally through intimate communications, physically through touching, and genitally through foreplay and the act of sexual intercourse. Sexuality and spirituality are interrelated in complex and multifaceted ways.

A homosexual orientation is to be distinguished from a homosexual act. A homosexual act is any sexual activity between two individuals of the same gender. A homosexual orientation describes an individual whose sexual drive is directed toward an individual of the same gender. Thus a homosexual orientation involves emotional attractions toward the same gender and may or may not involve homosexual acts. Most sociologists agree that the concept of homosexual orientation was not present in the culture of biblical times (Greenberg, 1988). Most evangelical psychologists believe that most individuals who own a homosexual orientation have not made an initial choice to direct their sexuality toward their own gender." (Benner and Hill 1985, 1999, 572)

Spiritual brothers and sisters struggle with same-sex attraction, who find the term homosexual repulsive when applied to those who struggle with same-sex attraction. Therefore, we will just stick with the phrase same-sex attraction and qualify whether we are referring to sexually active or inactive. Before moving on, let us take a moment to consider how we came to be in this fallen, imperfect condition.

Human Rebellion Excursion

God's intention was that his first couple, Adam, and Eve, were to procreate and cultivate the Garden of Eden until it covered the entire earth, filled with perfect humans worshipping him. – Genesis 1:28

If the first couple had not rebelled, they and their offspring could have lived forever. – Genesis 2:15-17

One of the angels in heaven (who became Satan) abused his free will. (James 1:14-15) He chose to rebel against God, and he used a lowly serpent to contribute to Adam and Eve abusing their free will and disobeying God, believing they did not need him and could walk on their own. – Genesis 3:1-6; Job 1-2.

God removed the rebellious Adam and Eve from the Garden of Eden. (Gen 3:23-24) The first human couple had children, but they all grew old and eventually died (Gen. 3:19; Rom 5:12), just as the animals died. – Ecclesiastes 3:18-20

Again, repetition for emphasis, Genesis 6:5 (AT) tells us just before the flood of Noah that "the wickedness of man on earth was great, and the whole bent of his thinking was never anything but evil." After the flood, God said of man, "the bent of man's mind may be evil from his very youth." (Gen 8:21, AT) Jeremiah 10:23 tells us "that it is not in man who walks to direct his steps." Jeremiah 17:9 says that "The heart is deceitful above all things, and desperately sick; who can understand it?" Yes, man was not designed to walk on his own. However, man was also not designed with absolute free will, but free will under the sovereignty of his Creator. Imperfect man is mentally bent toward wickedness, fleshly desires, to which Satan has set up this world, so it caters to the fallen flesh. "For all that is in the world, the desires of the flesh and the desires of the eyes and pride of life, is not from the Father but is from the world."—1 John 2:16.

Getting back to Genesis 1:27 that says, "God created man in his own image, in the image of God he created him; male and female he created them," meaning that man is born with a moral nature, which creates within him a conscience that reflects God's moral values. (Rom. 2:14-15) It acts as a moral law within us. However, it has an opponent as fallen man also possesses the "law of sin," 'missing the mark of perfection,' the natural desire toward wickedness. Listen to the internal battle of the apostle Paul. – Romans 6:12; 7:22-23.

Romans 7:21-23 Updated American Standard Version (UASV)

²¹ I find then the law in me that when I want to do right, that evil is present in me. ²² For I delight in the law of God according to the inner man, ²³ but I see a different law in my members, warring against the law of my mind [Paul's desire to obey God's law] and taking me captive in the law of sin [what wars against the law of his mind] which is in my members.

Here Paul uses the law motif to illustrate from another angle the conflict he experiences. Two laws are mentioned: **the law of my mind** (his desire to obey God's law), and **the law of sin** (that which wars against the law of his mind). He states a principle by which these two laws conflict with one another: **when I want to do good, evil is right there with me**. All of us can identify with the apostle's succinct summary of the spiritual experience.

Not only Paul, but all believers, have "left undone those things which we ought to have done." And as the Anglican

33

confession rightly concludes ("there is no health in us"), Paul is about to explode with his own spiritual diagnosis.[42]

However, there is hope,

Romans 7:24-25 Updated American Standard Version (UASV)

[24] Wretched man that I am! Who will deliver me from this body of death? [25] Thanks be to God through Jesus Christ our Lord! So then, I myself serve the law of God with my mind, but with my flesh, I serve the law of sin.

One of the results of the gospel is that it delivers us from the condemnation of the law. "Of what use then is the Law? To lead us to Christ, the Truth—to waken in our minds a sense of what our deepest nature, the presence, namely, of God *in* us, requires of us—to let us know, in part by failure, that the purest efforts of will of which we are capable cannot lift us up even to the abstaining from wrong to our neighbor" (George MacDonald, in Lewis, p. 20).

The law did its perfect work in the apostle Paul, reviving his soul (Ps. 19:7a). It convicted him of his sin and showed him that the only deliverance for him was Jesus Christ. No wonder Paul could call the law a "tutor to lead us to Christ, that we may be justified by faith" (Gal. 3:24, NASB). That is exactly what the law did for him. Once delivered from the law, Paul was able to serve the ends of the law—righteousness—in the power of the Holy Spirit (Rom. 7:6).

Paul summarizes the entire chapter—the conflict of the believer that causes him or her to remain dependent upon the Spirit—in the final verse. When it is Paul the believer talking, he makes himself a **slave to God's law**. But when his sinful capacity speaks out, he is **a slave to the law of sin**. As mentioned in this chapter earlier, it is a shame that chapter divisions in our Bibles cause us to "stop" at certain points in the consideration of the text. While this is a logical point in the flow of Paul's thought for a pause, Romans 7 and 8 should be read together. Immediately, Paul moves from wretchedness to victory in declaring that the law of the Spirit of life in Christ Jesus has set him "free from the law of sin and death" (Rom. 8:2). The gospel is indeed good news,

---

[42] (Boa and Kruidenier, Holman New Testament Commentary: Romans, Vol. 6 2000, 231)

delivering the believer from death by law to life by grace through the Spirit.[43]

From the Old Person to the New Person

The apostle Paul wrote,

1 Corinthians 2:14 Updated American Standard Version (UASV)

[14] But the natural man does not accept the things of the Spirit of God, for they are foolishness to him, and he is not able to understand them, because they are examined spiritually.

This does not in and of itself mean that the unbeliever cannot understand God's Word as they can. Rather, some unbelievers see it as foolish; therefore, they reject it and refuse to apply it in their lives. What we are addressing is what Paul meant by the natural man. This is one with no spiritual life, in that he follows the desires of his fallen flesh, setting aside God and his Word as mere foolishness. Paul informs us of hope that these unbelievers fail to find.

Ephesians 4:23 Updated American Standard Version (UASV)

[23] and to be renewed in the spirit of your minds,

We are **to be made new in the attitude of our minds**. How? You are what you think. You move in the direction of what you put into your mind and what you allow your mind to dwell on. So if you are not what you want to be, then you must begin to think differently. If you are to think differently, you must put into your mind that which you want to become. If you do, the Holy Spirit will use it to change you to become what you want to be. If you don't, you will never be what you want to be. It all depends on what you put into your mind. This is what it means to be made new in the attitude of your mind.[44]

Paul goes on to say,

Ephesians 4:24 Updated American Standard Version (UASV)

[24] and put on the new man, the one created according to the likeness of God in righteousness and loyalty of the truth.

---

[43] IBID., 232

[44] (Anders, Holman New Testament Commentary: vol. 8, Galatians, Ephesians, Philippians, Colossians 1999)

We are **to put on the new self**. This means, we are to allow the new self to govern our activities. We are to begin living the lifestyle that corresponds to who we have become in Christ. This new holy self shows we are maturing, growing in unity with the body, and doing our part of the body's work.[45]

Colossians 3:9-10 Updated American Standard Version (UASV)

⁹ Do not lie to one another, seeing that you have put off the old man[46] with its practices ¹⁰ and have put on the new man[47] who is being renewed through accurate knowledge[48] according to the image of the one who created him,

Perverted passions, hot tempers, and sharp tongues are to be removed as part of the life-transformation process. These things, along with **[lying] to each other**, are not appropriate behavior for our new life in Christ. The remnants of the former lifestyle are to be discarded **since [we] have taken off [our] old self with its practices**. What is the **old self** (literally "old man") and the **new self** (literally "the new")? The "old man" refers to more than an individual condition ("sinful nature") and also has a corporate aspect. The corporate aspect of "the new" (man) is unmistakably seen in verse 11. What has been **put off** and what has been **put on?** Our former associations, the old humanity has been **put off**, and we now have a new association, the new community. As members of the new community, we are to conduct ourselves in ways which will enhance harmony in the community. Notice how the sins mentioned in the previous verses disrupt community and damage human relationships.[49]

Romans 12:2 Updated American Standard Version (UASV)

² And do not be conformed to this world, but be transformed by the renewing of your mind, so that you may prove what the will of God is, that which is good and acceptable[50] and perfect.

---

[45] IBID.

[46] Or *old person*

[47] Or *new person*

[48] *Epignosis* is a strengthened or intensified form of *gnosis* (*epi*, meaning "additional"), meaning, "true," "real," "full," "complete" or "accurate," depending upon the context. Paul and Peter alone use *epignosis*.

[49] IBID., 330

[50] Or *well-pleasing*

In the beginning of a person's introduction to the good news, he will take in knowledge of the Scriptures (1 Tim. 2:3-4), which if his heart is receptive, he will begin to apply them in his life, taking off the old person and putting on the new person. (Eph. 4:22-24) Seeing how the Scriptures have begun to alter his life, he will start to have a genuine faith over the things that he has learned (Heb. 11:6), repenting of his sins. (Acts 17:30-31) He will turn around his life, and his sins will be blotted out. (Acts 3:19) At some point, he will go to the Father in prayer, telling him that he is dedicating his life to him, to carry out his will and purposes. (Matt. 16:24; 22:37) This regeneration is the Holy Spirit working in his life, giving him a new nature, placing him on the path to salvation. – 2 Corinthians 5:17. (Andrews 2013, 17)

Indeed, we may have thought this long excursion had us off in the weeds. However, it seemed important that the reader understands that humanities fall into sin and exactly what that means to appreciate what is about to be said. Every physical, mental, and emotional issue that has fallen upon man directly results from our imperfection, something that God did not intend but has allowed to happen as an object lesson (See the Chapter Why Has God Permitted Wickedness and Suffering). This means mental disorders like depression, bipolar, schizophrenia, anxiety disorder, obsessive-compulsive disorder, and so on result from inherited imperfection. This would also apply to persons who struggle with same-sex attraction.

Some argue that same-sex attraction is brought about through socialization. Somebody acquires a personality or traits through their background (nurture), impacted by family, friends, school, work, and so on. Others would argue that same-sex attraction is brought about because one is genetically predisposed (nature).[51] We will take on the science of such an issue herein but not as a scientist.

Let me just say that it is likely a mixture of both. Let us take a young woman (true story)[52] who was in an abusive marriage, mentally, emotionally, and physically. We will call her **Sandy**.[53] She had a very close friend (we will

---

[51] "A **genetic predisposition** (sometimes also called **genetic** susceptibility) is an increased likelihood of developing a particular disease based on a person's **genetic** makeup. A **genetic predisposition** results from specific **genetic** variations that are often inherited from a parent." – What does it mean to have a genetic predisposition to a ..,

http://ghr.nlm.nih.gov/handbook/mutationsanddisorders/predisposition (accessed April 16, 2016).

[52] The account is true, but the names are changed.

[53] Names in this book have been changed.

call **Cindy**), who also suffered from the ravages of an abusive husband. One night, after a very trying week, they find themselves alone, sitting on a couch, talking to each other as they watch a movie. Through tears and a broken heart, they unloaded as to just how bad it is. Soon, Sandy goes into an uncontrollable sob, so Cindy holds her in her arms, stroking her hair, comforting her with her soft voice. After a while, the sobbing stops, and Cindy brushes Sandy's tears away. Cindy then leans in and starts kissing Sandy, and Sandy does not pull away.

This begins a five-year same-sex relationship until Sandy feels wrong and decides to return to her faith. Sandy was not actually attracted to women; she did not have same-sex attraction (nurture). However, her childhood abuse, coupled with a highly abusive husband and a loving and comforting friend, led to her finding comfort in this relationship. On the other hand, Cindy was and is a person that has same-sex attraction (nature). She entered the marriage with her husband because she was trying to avoid the stigma of being of the same-sex attraction. She went to the same Christian congregation as Sandy. Here could be a real-life case of one who was socialized into a same-sex relationship and genetically predisposed to a same-sex relationship.

This author would argue that science is irrelevant to the Christian faith. Let us err on the side of those who say that, for some, it is genetic, and they are predisposed toward same-sex attraction. If we concede this, it does nothing to remove the Bible's position on same-sex relationships. Remember, the Bible says that we are all mentally bent toward wickedness. We should understand that some lean toward different things in this mental bent, and others lean heavily in other directions. By tentatively erring on this side of some being genetically predisposed, we can better help them and better understand their struggles. Lastly, because we accept genetic predisposition, this does not exclude their gaining control over their body and mind and being able to take off the old person and put on the new person. Moreover, it does not exclude that many same-sex attraction cases are socialized.

What is the Bible's View of Homosexuality?

What is said about homosexuality in the New Testament is grounded in what had already been said in the Old Testament. We have already discussed Genesis 1:26-27, which states that humans were made in the image of God. "The crowning point of creation, a living human, was made in God's image to rule creation. Our image . . . likeness. This speaks of the creation of Adam in terms that are uniquely personal. It establishes a personal relationship between God and man that does not exist with any other aspect of creation.

It is the very thing that makes humanity different from every other created animal. It explains why the Bible places so much stress on God's hands-on creation of Adam. He fashioned this creature in a special way—to bear the stamp of His own likeness. It suggests that God was, in essence, the pattern for the personhood of man. The image of God is personhood, and personhood can function only in the context of relationships. Man's capacity for intimate, personal relationships needed fulfillment. Most important, man was designed to have a personal relationship with God. It is impossible to divorce this truth from the fact that man is an ethical creature. All true relationships have ethical ramifications. It is at this point that God's communicable attributes come into play. Man is a living being capable of embodying God's communicable attributes (cf. 9:6; Rom. 8:29; Col. 3:10; James 3:9). In his rational life, he was like God in that he could reason and had intellect, will, and emotion. In the moral sense, he was like God because he was good and sinless."[54]

Genesis 2:18-25 Updated American Standard Version (UASV)

[18] Then Jehovah God said, "It is not good for the man to be alone; I will make him a helper for him.[55] [19] And out of the ground Jehovah God formed every beast of the field, and every bird of the heavens; and brought them to the man to see what he would call them; and whatsoever the man called every living soul, that was its name. [20] And the man gave names to all cattle, and to the birds of the heavens, and to every beast of the field; but for man there was found no helper as a counterpart of him. [21] So Jehovah God caused a deep sleep to fall upon the man, and he slept; then he took one of his ribs and closed up the flesh at that place. [22] And the rib that Jehovah God had taken from the man he made into a woman and brought her to the man.

[23] Then the man said,

"This at last is bone of my bones
and flesh of my flesh;
she shall be called Woman,
because she was taken out of Man."

[24] Therefore a man shall leave his father and his mother and be joined to his wife, and they shall be as one flesh. [25] And the man and his wife were both naked and were not ashamed.

In Genesis 2:18–25 we find that there are physical differences between man and woman, yet God mat them compatible and complementary with

---

[54] MacArthur, John (2005-05-09). *The MacArthur Bible Commentary* (Kindle Locations 1924-1933). Thomas Nelson. Kindle Edition.

[55] Lit., "as his opposite;" *counterpart or complement*, something that completes or perfects him

one another. The man produces while the woman bears children, which is why we find Adam saying of Eve, "This at last is bone of my bones and flesh of my flesh," while God inspired Moses to say that "they [man and woman] shall be as one flesh." We find the foundation of how men and women were meant to be, a model, example, pattern, or standard as to their sexual relations. Therefore, God intended that marriage and sexual relations were/are to be between one man and one woman. Moreover, marriage and sexual relations between two persons of the same-sex would be contrary to God's personality, standards, ways, and will and purposes (sin) and contrary to nature.

Genesis 9:18-28 – If it is Ham that saw Noah's nakedness, why is Canaan the one getting cursed?

Genesis 9:18 Updated American Standard Version (UASV)

Prophecies about Descendants of Noah

18 The sons of Noah who went forth from the ark were Shem, Ham, and Japheth. (Ham was the father of Canaan.) 19 These three were the sons of Noah, and from these the whole earth was scattered.[56]

20 Noah began to be a man of the soil, and he planted a vineyard. 21 He drank of the wine and became drunk and uncovered himself inside his tent. 22 And Ham, the father of Canaan, saw the nakedness of his father and told his two brothers outside. 23 Then Shem and Japheth took a garment, and laid it on both their shoulders, and walked backward and covered the nakedness of their father; and their faces were turned backward,[57] and they did not see their father's nakedness. 24 When Noah awoke from his wine,[58] he knew what his youngest son had done to him. 25 And he said,

"Cursed be Canaan;
a slave of slaves[59] shall he be to his brothers."

26 He also said,

"Blessed be Jehovah, the God of Shem;
and let Canaan be his slave.

---

[56] I.e., *populated*

[57] I.e., *turned away*

[58] I.e., *drunkenness*

[59] Or *servant of servants*

40

²⁷ "May God enlarge Japheth,
and let him dwell in the tents of Shem;
and let Canaan be his slave."

²⁸ Noah lived three hundred and fifty years after the flood. ²⁹ And all the days of Noah were nine hundred and fifty years, and he died.

Commenting on Genesis 9:24, which states that when Noah awoke from his wine he "got to know what his youngest son had done to him," a footnote in Rotherham's translation says, "Undoubtedly Canaan, and not Ham: Shem and Japheth, for their piety, are blessed; Canaan, for some unnamed baseness, is cursed; Ham, for his neglect, is neglected." Similarly, a Jewish publication, *The Pentateuch and Haftorahs*, suggests that the brief narrative "refers to some abominable deed in which Canaan seems to have been implicated." (Edited by J. H. Hertz, London, 1972, p. 34) In addition, after noting that the Hebrew word translated "son" in verse 24 may mean "grandson," this source states, "The reference is evidently to Canaan." The Soncino Chumash also points out that some believe Canaan "indulged a perverted lust upon [Noah]," and that the expression "youngest son" refers to Canaan, who was the youngest son of Ham. – Edited by A. Cohen, London, 1956, p. 47.

As is generally the case, context can clear the muddied waters, to see more clearly. We should mention here that there is no explicit evidence for the inference that we are about to suggest, so we are not being dogmatic about our understanding.

Genesis 9:18 Updated American Standard Version (UASV)

¹⁸ The sons of Noah who went forth from the ark were Shem, Ham, and Japheth. (Ham was the father of Canaan.)

One must ask why the account has an abrupt interruption here, with a parenthetical of introducing Canaan, before covering the drunkenness of Noah.

Genesis 9:22 Updated American Standard Version (UASV)

²² And Ham, the father of Canaan, saw the nakedness of his father and told his two brothers outside.

Here again, the account is pulling us back to Canaan. As the actions of Ham are being disclosed, the account goes out of its way to emphasize Canaan, saying "Ham, the father of Canaan." Both of these seem to imply that Canaan is an essential part of understanding the account.

We can accept that the expression "saw the nakedness of his father" as a means of expressing some kind of perversion or abuse on Noah by Canaan. If we turn to Leviticus, you will find that similar expressions are used in reference to sexual sins and incest. (Lev. 18:6-19; 20:17) Therefore, it is possible that Canaan committed some type of sexual abuse on the unconscious Noah, to which Ham had knowledge and did not take measures to prevent or discipline if it was after the fact. Worse still, he made this known to the brothers, which brought more embarrassment and shame on Noah.

Then, there is the matter of the curse itself. "Cursed be Canaan; a servant of servants shall he be to his brothers." (Gen. 9:25) There is no biblical evidence that Canaan was ever a servant to his uncles Shem or Japheth. However, we are dealing with Jehovah God, who possesses foreknowledge. Moreover, the curse is in the Word of God and thus shows that it was divinely inspired and must therefore come true. We must keep in mind that God does not disfavor a person or people without a justifiable reason behind it. Is it possible that Canaan was already acting on some type of sinful leanings, such as same-sex attraction, and that Jehovah foresaw the outcome of that within the Canaanites, descendants of Canaan?

If we recall, Jehovah could read the heart-attitude of Cain and had warned him of the results if he did not change his disposition. (Gen. 4:3-7) In addition, God was able to discern the level of wickedness that was to be in the preflood population. (Gen 6:5) Moreover, God was able to detect the unborn Jacob and Esau's genetic bent while they were still in the womb. – Genesis 25:23.

We see the justifiableness of God's curse on Canaan in the history of his descendants. They were so immoral that archaeologists who dug up their area were surprised that God had not destroyed them sooner. (Gen. 15:15-16) They too had a lust for the same sex. The Bible is right alongside secular history in exposing the sordid past of the Canaanites. The curse was fulfilled about eight centuries after Noah uttered the words when the Israelites conquered the land of Canaan. Later too, they would be subjected even further by the descendants of Japheth, by way of Medo-Persia, Greece, and Rome.

Leviticus 18:22 – Since "Christ is the end of the [Mosaic] law" (Rom. 10:4), does this include homosexuality?

Leviticus 18:22 Updated American Standard Version (UASV)

22 You shall not lie with a male as you lie down with a woman; it is an abomination.

The law against homosexuality is in the heart of the Mosaic Law, the book of Leviticus. This is the book of laws on the seriousness of sin and the importance of being holy. We know that the civil and ceremonial laws were done away with, as Jesus "canceled out the certificate of debt consisting of decrees against [the Israelites], which was hostile to [the Israelites]; and He has taken it out of the way, having nailed it to the cross." (Col. 2:13-14, NASB) Since the civil and ceremonial laws of the Old Testament were removed from the law of Christ[60] (Gal. 6:2), does this mean that they are not under any laws? No, as Jesus introduced "a new covenant," while 'making the first one obsolete,' based on his perfect human life. Christians are under this "new covenant" and are to be obedient to Christian laws. (Heb. 8:7-13; Lu 22:20) However, it must be remembered that many of the Christian Laws have been taken from the Mosaic Law. Christians are urged to "fulfill the law of Christ," as opposed to the civil and ceremonial laws of the Hebrew Scriptures. (Gal. 6:2) Notice how Jesus took parts of the Mosaic Law and clarified the deeper sense of them.

"You Have Heard That It Was Said"

Matthew 5:17 Updated American Standard Version (UASV)

[17] Think not that I came to destroy the law or

Counsel on Anger

[21] "**You have heard that it was said** to the ancients, 'You shall not murder; and whoever murders will be liable to judgment.' [22] **But I say to you** that everyone who is angry with his brother will be liable to judgment; whoever says to his brother, 'You fool,'[61] will be brought before the Sanhedrin;[62] and whoever says, 'You fool!' will be liable to the fire of Gehenna.[63]

Counsel on Adultery

[27] "**You have heard that it was said**, 'You shall not commit adultery';[64] [28] **but I say to you** that everyone who looks at a woman with lust[65] for her has already committed adultery with her in his heart.

---

[60] "**The law of Christ**" (ὁ νόμος τοῦ Χριστοῦ) is a New Testament phrase found only in the Pauline Epistles at Galatians 6:2 and parenthetically (ἔννομος Χριστῷ "being under the **law** to **Christ**") at 1 Corinthians 9:21.

[61] Gr *Raca to*, an Aramaic term of contempt

[62] The Jewish supreme court, which held life and death over the people in ancient Jerusalem before 70 C.E.

[63] *geenna* 12x pr. *the valley of Hinnom*, south of Jerusalem, once celebrated for the horrid worship of Moloch, and afterwards polluted with every species of filth, as well as the carcasses of animals, and dead bodies of malefactors; to consume which, in order to avert the pestilence which such a mass of corruption would occasion, constant fires were kept burning—MCEDONTW

[64] Ex. 20:14; Deut. 5:17

[65] ἐπιθυμία [*Epithumia*] to strongly desire to have what belongs to someone else and/or to engage in an activity which is morally wrong—'to covet, to lust, evil desires, lust, desire.'– GELNTBSD

Counsel on Divorce

31 "**It was said**, 'Whoever divorces his wife away, let him give her a certificate of divorce';[66] 32 **but I say to you** that everyone who divorces his wife, except on the ground of sexual immorality, makes her commit adultery; and whoever marries a divorced woman commits adultery.

Counsel on Oaths

33 "Again **you have heard that it was said** to those of old, 'You shall not swear falsely, but shall perform to the Lord what you have sworn.'[67] 34 **But I say to you**, Do not swear at all, either by heaven, for it is the throne of God, 35 or by the earth, for it is his footstool of his feet, or by Jerusalem, for it is the city of the great King. 36 Nor shall you make an oath by your head, for you cannot make one hair white or black. 37 But let your word 'yes' be 'yes,' and your 'no' be 'no'; anything more than this is from the evil one.

Counsel on Retaliation

38 "**You have heard that it was said**, 'An eye for an eye, and a tooth for a tooth.'[68] 39 **But I say to you**, Do not resist the one who is evil; but whoever slaps you on your right cheek, turn the other to him also.

Counsel on Love of Enemies

43 "**You have heard that it was said**, 'You shall love your neighbor[69] and hate your enemy.'[70] 44 **But I say to you**, love your enemies and pray for those who persecute you, 45 so that you may be sons of your Father who is in heaven

We notice that Jesus referred to parts of the Mosaic Law with the phrase "**You have heard that it was said.**" This was followed by a law or better yet the Pharisaical view[71] of that law, and then he closed with the phrase "**But I say to you.**" This was followed by a deeper understanding of the law, the moral value behind the law, the spirit behind the law. The deeper spirit behind the law will see continued anger as murder. The deeper spirit behind

---

[66] Deut. 24:1

[67] Lev. 19:12

[68] Ex. 21:24; Lev. 24:20

[69] Lev. 19:18

[70] A twisting of Deut. 23:3–6

[71] Pharisaical righteously obsessed with rules: acting with hypocrisy, self-righteousness, or obsessiveness with regard to the strict adherence to rules and formalities

the law will see continued lustful thinking as adultery. The deeper spirit behind the law will see divorcing over nothing as leading to adulterous remarriage. The deeper spirit behind the law will see tiresome-frivolous oaths to be pointless. The deeper spirit behind the law will see the wisdom of mildness over retaliation. The deeper spirit behind the law will see godly love that knows no bounds.

Finally, there are two important points to be made. First, Even though Christians are not under the Mosaic Law today, the divine principles behind them are still of great value to us because the spirit behind them will never change. Second, the moral laws of the Mosaic law were not done away with (nailed to the cross) because they are a part of God's character and are eternal. Just because the moral law, prohibiting homosexuality, is found in the book of Leviticus, where we also find many ceremonial laws, this does not mean that it too passed away.

If one argues that the moral law of homosexuality is to be removed because it is found in the book of Leviticus because much of the ceremonial and civil laws therein were abolished; they would have to argue against rape, incest, and bestiality as well. (Lev. 18:6-14, 22-23) In addition, we would have to abolish lying and theft (Lev. 19:11), oppressing your neighbor (Lev. 19:13), slandering your neighbor (19:16), hating your fellow man (Lev. 19:17), taking vengeance, nor bearing a grudge (Lev. 19:18), avoiding unjust balances (Lev. 19:36), sacrificing your children (Lev. 20:1-5), and committing adultery (Lev. 20:10). Moreover, Leviticus is quoted in the New Testament.

Leviticus	New Testament
Leviticus 19:2 Updated American Standard Version (UASV) 2 "Speak to all the congregation of the sons of Israel and say to them, 'You shall be holy, for I Jehovah your God am holy.	**1 Peter 1:16** Updated American Standard Version (UASV) 16 because it is written, "You shall be holy, for I am holy."
Leviticus 19:18 Updated American Standard Version (UASV) 18 You shall not take vengeance, nor bear any grudge against the sons of your people, but	**Matthew 22:39** Updated American Standard Version (UASV) 39 The second, like it, is this: 'You must love your neighbor as yourself.'

you shall love your neighbor as yourself; I am Jehovah.	
Leviticus 26:12 Updated American Standard Version (UASV) ¹² And I will also walk among you and be your God, and you shall be my people.	**2 Corinthians 6:16** Updated American Standard Version (UASV) ¹⁶ And what agreement has the temple of God with idols? For we are the temple of the living God; just as God said, "I will dwell in them and I will walk among them, and I will be their God, and they shall be my people.

There can be no excuse that this moral law was only applicable to the Jewish people because it is applied to the Gentiles in Romans 1:26. Moreover, we just spoke of God condemning the Canaanites specifically for their homosexuality. (Gen. 18:1-3, 25) This moral law is specifically forbidden in the New Testament. – Romans 1:26-27; 1 Corinthians 6:9; 1 Timothy 1:10; and Jude 7.

The Bible and Sexuality [Excursion]

From the earliest times, God acknowledged the existence of and controlled the conduct of human sexuality. The sexual motivation comes from the inner nature of man, and it forms the drive to populate the earth (Gen. 1:28). Men and women can fulfill this mandate with the utmost fulfillment, provided they follow the teachings of the Bible on sexual conduct. Sarah even used the term pleasure to describe the sexual act (Gen. 18:12). God intended the physical union between man and woman to represent a holy intimacy, at times describing the very act as "knowing" the partner (Num. 31:17). Such knowledge assumes a deep personal connection between the husband and wife that extends far beyond the physical realm but includes the entire person.

God himself describes the sexual partners as forming "one flesh" (Gen. 2:24; Mark 10:7–8; Eph. 5:31). The man who engages a prostitute in intercourse becomes "one with her in body" (1 Cor.

6:16), a practice God commands us to "flee" lest we sin against our own bodies (1 Cor. 6:18). God intended the normal sexual function to include a commitment and love that went beyond sexual fulfillment.

The Old Testament required young women to remain virgins until marriage on penalty of death (Deut. 22:13–24). While God did not repeat the same restrictions for males, he implied it by prohibiting fornication (Exod. 22:16–17) and punishing it with varying penalties. Adultery was strictly forbidden, and this comprised one of the Ten Commandments (Exod. 20:14). God forbade any species of incest, physical unions between family members, although some people in the Bible ignored such warnings. Lot, seduced by his daughters into a drunken stupor, lost his powers of judgment and impregnated them (Gen. 19:30–38). Reuben slept with his father Jacob's concubine (Gen. 35:22), and Judah had relations with his daughter-in-law Tamar (Gen. 38).

Jesus and the apostles shed the clearest light of all on this delicate issue. Jesus redefined popular notions of sin by discovering its origins: it resides in the human heart. Consequently, a man commits adultery not only by engaging in unlawful intercourse with his neighbor's wife but by harboring such desires in his heart (Matt. 5:27–30). Luke faithfully records the decrees of the early church that, among other things, prohibited sexual immorality (Acts 15:20). Paul constructed an elaborate theology of marriage, detailing both its positive privileges and strict parameters (1 Cor. 6:13–20; 7:1–40; Eph. 5:3–7; 1 Thess. 4:3).

Finally, the Bible forbids homosexuality of any sort (Lev. 18:22; 20:13; Rom. 1:26–27). The modern term sodomy derived its name from the failed attempts of the inhabitants of Sodom to rape the visiting angels (Gen. 19:4–11). The degree to which a society gives way to such practices is a good gauge to measure not only the nation's separation from God but also its prospects for long-term survival (see Lev. 18:24–25; cp. Gen. 15:16). The only island of sanity we find in a sea without sexual standards is the comprehensive biblical instruction on sexual behavior. On a positive and hopeful note, many whom God saved from pagan and hedonistic lifestyles have found peace, purpose, and fulfillment in Christ. God did a marvelous work in their lives and renewed them in the way they approach these matters. God leaves no one outside of the reach of his gracious provision in Christ, and many who once sought meaning in the empty relationships now find complete fulfillment in following the Bible's prescription for healthy and satisfying sexual behavior.[72]

Earlier, we read the Apostle Paul's words, "Do not be conformed to this world, but **be transformed by the renewal of your mind**, that by testing you may discern what is the will of God, what is good and acceptable and perfect." How can we renew our mind? The center of consciousness stores knowledge and can think, understand, and reason. Well, if it is the mindset of the world, which can get us askew, we must take in knowledge from another source, creating a different mindset. Paul made this very clear to the Ephesians when he gave them instructions for Christian living to build a new life. Paul said, 'As a follower of the Lord, I order you to stop living like stupid, godless people. Their minds are in the dark, and they are stubborn and ignorant and have missed out on the life that comes from God. They no longer have any feelings about what is right, and they are so greedy that they do all kinds of indecent things.' (Eph. 4:17-19, CEV) Because of their callused hearts, the god of this world blinds these so that the truth cannot get through.

Leviticus 18:22-24 – Is the Curse of Barrenness Behind God's Condemnation of Homosexuality?

Leviticus 18:22-24 Updated American Standard Version (UASV)

[22] You shall not lie with a male as you lie down with a woman; it is an abomination. [23] And you shall not lie with any animal and so make yourself unclean with it, neither shall any woman stand before an animal to lie with it:[73] it is perversion.

[24] 'Do not defile yourselves by any of these things; for by all these the nations which I am casting out before you have become defiled.

Leviticus 20:13 Updated American Standard Version (UASV)

[13] If a man lies down with a male as one lies down with a woman, both of them have committed a detestable thing; they shall surely be put to death. Their own blood is upon them.

The inability to conceive children is conveyed by the Hebrew words *aqar* ("barren," Gen. 11:30) and *galmud* ("barren," i.e. Isa 49:21; Job 15:34). Proverbs 30:16 gives its reader four examples of greed, "Sheol, and **the barren womb**, Earth that is never satisfied with water, And fire that never

---

[72] Anders, Max; Martin, Glen (2002-07-01). Holman Old Testament Commentary - Exodus, Leviticus, Numbers (pp. 227-229). B&H Publishing. Kindle Edition.

[73] A woman must not offer herself to a male animal to have intercourse with it. (NLT); A woman shall not stand before an animal to copulate with it (LEB)

says, 'Enough.'" At each start of humanity, one perfect (Adam and Eve), one imperfect (Noah and family), God gave one specific command.

God had commanded both Adam and Eve as well as Noah and his family, "Be fruitful and multiply, and fill the earth" (Gen. 1:28; 9:7) In ancient times, a childless or barren womb, being unable to conceive, was viewed as a reproach, an illness, a punishment, one of the greatest calamities. "When Rachel saw that she bore Jacob no children, she became jealous of her sister [Leah]; and she said to Jacob, "Give me children, or else I die." (Gen. 30:1, NASB) Of course, God had the power of making a woman with natural barrenness able to conceive: Sarah (Gen. 11:30; 17:19; 21:1, 2), Rebekah (Gen. 25:21), Samson's mother (Judges 13:2, 3), Hannah (1 Sam. 1:10, 11; 2:5), a Shunammite woman (2 Ki 4:14-17), and Elizabeth (Lu 1:7, 36).

There are no Scriptures, which would indicate that homosexuality was sinful because of the inability to conceive. Moreover, "if homosexuals were punished because they were barren, then why were they put to death? The dead can't have any more children! Since it is against the desires of homosexuals, heterosexual marriage would have been a more appropriate punishment!"[74]

In addition, homosexuality was not just prohibited among the Jews, as all the nations (non-Jews) of the land of Canaan, who were being cast out, had become defiled with such homosexual practices. The Jewish people were not blessed based on their ability to have children but rather on their obedience to God.

Lastly, barrenness could not have been a divine curse; otherwise, singleness would have been sinful. However, both Jesus and the apostle Paul recommended singleness for those who could exercise self-control over themselves to carry out their discipleship unhindered. – Matthew 19:11-12; 1 Corinthians 7:8.

Clearly, the whole of the Old Testament condemns and prohibits homosexuality. As we have just read in Leviticus 18:22 and 20:13, homosexual relations are condemned and prohibited. Some try to argue that these verses only refer to male homosexual relations, as though God would condemn and prohibit male homosexual relations but not female homosexual relations. The Bible uses the male gender about God and his Son and various angels and demons. The Bible is a book based on the male gender because Adam was created first; he was the head of humanity. This is not to say that men are superior to women, but women are subordinate and in

---

[74] Thomas Howe; Norman L. Geisler. The Big Book of Bible Difficulties: Clear and Concise Answers from Genesis to Revelation

49

subjection to men. The Bible refers to the male gender when the principle, rule, or law is also applicable to women as well. The Creator of all things chose the setting, the language, and time in which his Word was to be introduced to man. In biblical times, speakers would address a mixed group of believers with the greeting "brothers." What have gender-inclusive translations (e.g., CEV, NLT, TEV, etc.) have been doing over the past seventy years?

The English Standard Version makes more boasts about the importance of literal translation and yet violates that philosophy in at least four ways: (1) Crossway Bibles hired Bill Mounce, a proponent of dynamic equivalent translation as its chief translator. (2) It uses *essentially* literal to qualify its level of literalness. (3) It abandons the literal rendering far too many times to count. (4) It has joined the gender-neutral or gender-inclusive translations. For example, a literal translation (ASV, RSV, NASB, and UASV) will always uses the word man for the Greek *anthropos*, even when the context suggests that both men and women are in view. However, the ESV and other gender-inclusive translations will render such as people or others.

These gender-inclusive translators fail to understand this: to deviate, in any way, from the pattern, or likeness of how God brought his Word into existence, merely opens the Bible up to a book that reflects the age and time of its readers. If we allow the Bible to be altered because the progressive woman's movement feels offended by masculine language, it will not be long before the Bible gives way to the homosexual communities being offended by God's Words in the book of Romans and Corinthians; so modern translations will then tame that language, so as to not cause offense. I am certain that we thought that we would never see the day of two men or two women being married by priests, but that day has been upon us for some time now. In fact, the American government is debating whether to change the definition of marriage.

The point here is that Leviticus 18:22 and 20:13 may refer to **male** homosexual relations, but this is a reference to a male gender when the condemnation and prohibition are also applicable to women as well. It would be utterly ridiculous and willful ignorance to see it any other way. The act of homosexual relations in the Old Testament called for capital punishment. Some may argue that Christ and the New Testament authors lightened the sentence and stigma for such offenses against God. However, this is just not the case. Jesus is just as clear, but we will quote Paul, who said, God, would inflict "vengeance on those who do not know God and on those who do not obey the gospel of our Lord Jesus. They will suffer the punishment of eternal destruction." (2 Thess. 2:6-8) Some have tried to argue that Leviticus 18:22 and 20:13 is only speaking against cult prostitution. However, there is nothing

50

within the context of these Scriptures, which refers to any kind cultic activity. Moreover, homosexual relations are condemned and prohibited in both the Hebrew Scripture and the Greek New Testament. To try to argue that only some particular type of homosexual relations is prohibited is just another attempt at diverting attention or misleading.

Why did God Destroy Sodom and Gomorrah? What Was the Sin of Sodom and Gomorrah?

Those in support of the LBGT[75] community argue that Sodom and Gomorrah were not destroyed because of homosexuality, but rather it was the attempted homosexual rape. If this were the only verse in the Bible that spoke of homosexuality, one might be able to raise that argument. However, as we have already seen in the above, Genesis 9:18-28, where it was actually Canaan who saw the nakedness of Noah (homosexual act on Noah), for which he was prophetically cursed. Again, we see the justifiableness of God's curse on Canaan in the history of his descendants. Again, the point needs to be repeated. They were so immoral that archaeologists who dug up their area were surprised that God had not destroyed them sooner. (Gen. 15:15-16) They too had a lust for the same sex. The Bible is right alongside secular history in exposing the sordid past of the Canaanites. The curse was fulfilled about eight centuries after Noah uttered the words when the Israelites conquered the land of Canaan. The destruction of Sodom and Gomorrah was a precursor to the destruction that was to come at the hand of Joshua and the Israelite army. There is not one biblical reference that would suggest that homosexuality is simply an alternative lifestyle but rather a gross sin, detestable, contrary to nature, "shameful lusts" "indecent," a "perversion," and "the degrading of their bodies."

Moreover, the sin of homosexual relations is found all throughout Scripture. Others from the LBGT community try to argue that the custom and culture of the common hospitality of the Ancient Near Eastern family at the time, a lack of hospitality, and the ill-treatment of strangers, was the reason for the destruction of Sodom and Gomorrah. According to the Ancient Near East, it was a host's obligation to protect the guests in his home, defending them even to the point of death if necessary. Lot was certainly prepared to do that. Liberal scholarship being used as a tool argues that it was a lack of hospitality and the ill-treatment of strangers. The response is simple; Sodom and Gomorrah were destroyed for gross homosexual activity, which took place in a culture that greatly valued hospitality. Yes, the homosexual men of Sodom and Gomorrah were

---

[75] LGBT or GLBT is an initialism that stands for lesbian, gay, bisexual, and transgender.

violating the social customs as they sought to rape two angels that they believed to be two men.[76]

Thus, if Isaiah the prophet in chapter one refers to Sodom and Gomorrah as a bad example of evildoing and depravity, to help Judah appreciate just how far they had fallen, this does not negate the evil and depraved homosexual attempted rape of two men by the men of Sodom and Gomorrah. When the prophet Jeremiah compares the prophets of Jerusalem to the evil and wickedness of Sodom and Gomorrah (Jer. 23:14), this does not support the social customs argument, as the destruction of those two cities can be used analogously for evil and wickedness. The prophet Ezekiel compares Jerusalem to Samaria and Sodom, saying that Jerusalem was following Samaria and Sodom's way of life and their wicked customs. Soon, Jerusalem was more disgusting than they were. Again, we are talking about many disgusting things, of which homosexuality cannot be ruled out.

Nevertheless, Ezekiel was specifically talking about a failure to help the poor and needy. Are we to believe that God destroyed Israel by Babylon because they just did not give enough to the needy? Hardly, Jerusalem had perverted orgies under trees, worshipping false gods, offering their sons in sacrifice to Molech, committing homosexual acts, and many other disgusting, sinful things for centuries. The Old Testament prophets and the historical books list all of these things.

The argument is that it was the sin of being inhospitable, not homosexuality. Part of the LGBT argument is the fact that Lot implored that the males of the community 'not do this thing to these men, since they came under my roof for protection.' (Gen 19:8) They use this text to bolster their argument that it was a violation of the social norms of the day; the Ancient Near East had a custom that they would protect their guests, even a complete stranger with their own lives. They then use Ezekiel 16:49 to bolster that defense because Jerusalem is being compared to Sodom in order to Shame Jerusalem for her failure to "aid the poor and needy." Yes, the people of Sodom and Gomorrah were unhospitable, and verse 49 of Ezekiel chapter 16 mentions this as part of why they were judged adversely. However, the sin of Sodom and Gomorrah was selfishness, inhospitality, but also homosexuality. Verse 49 of Ezekiel chapter 16 is found within the context of 16:49-59, which shows the sin was their failure to aid the poor and needy (v 49), arrogance (v 50), and most of the text centers on engagement in detestable things, 'committed abominations before God.' (50-51) Abominations is the same word used in Leviticus 18:22, "You shall not lie with a male as one lies with a female; it is an abomination." Jesus' half-brother

---

[76] It was common for angels to materialize as men, never women.

Jude called the sin of 'Sodom and Gomorrah gross sexual immorality,' which is stated as "acted immorally and indulged in unnatural lust" in the Revised Standard Version (Jude 7).

Finally, the LGBT community and liberal scholars argue that the text of Genesis 19:5 does not even mention sexual acts. It reads, "They [men of Sodom and Gomorrah] called to Lot, 'Where are the men who came to you tonight? Bring them out to us, **that we may know them.**'" (Gen. 19:5, RSV) The Hebrew word for "know" *yada* occurs 956 times in the Old Testament and has a wide meaning. Its primary meaning was 'to get to know.'[77] Moreover, they would argue that the vast number of uses of *yada* in the Old Testament has nothing to do with sexual relations. However, the context determines the meaning because *yada* also has the meaning "to have sexual relations." The context of Sodom and Gomorrah, *yada*, clearly meant sexual relations. In Genesis, yada in almost every use between a man and a woman refers to sexual relations. Moreover, in the same chapter at Genesis 19:18, Lot says to the men surrounding his house, "I have two daughters who **have not known man**," *yada* being a clear reference to the fact that his daughters had not had sexual relations with a man. Lastly, if the context was that all of the males of Sodom and Gomorrah were simply coming to Lot's house "to get to know," i.e., 'to get acquainted with' the two men, why was lot offering his two virgin daughters in their place to appease the men's sexual appetite? The reason is simple; the men of Sodom and Gomorrah were homosexuals, who were going to rape these two men, clearly an abomination.

However, the LGBT community and liberal scholars must try to isolate a few verses that seem to support their argument of why Sodom and Gomorrah were destroyed. Certainly, the people of Sodom and Gomorrah were guilty of more than homosexuality, and they can be used as an example for these other wicked behaviors as well. Even Jesus used the people of Sodom as an example of being inhospitable to strangers. However, this does not negate the fact that the inhospitableness was a community of homosexual men trying to rape two angels that they believed to be men at the time of the destruction. However, one problem exists for the liberal scholars, Jude, Jesus half-brother, writing under inspiration tells us exactly why Sodom and Gomorrah were destroyed. He wrote, "Just as Sodom and Gomorrah and the cities around them, since they in the same way as these indulged in gross

---

[77] William D. Mounce, *Mounce's Complete Expository Dictionary of Old & New Testament Words* (Grand Rapids, MI: Zondervan, 2006), 947.

Robert L. Thomas, *New American Standard Hebrew-Aramaic and Greek Dictionaries : Updated Edition* (Anaheim: Foundation Publications, Inc., 1998).

R. Laird Harris, Gleason L. Archer Jr., and Bruce K. Waltke, eds., *Theological Wordbook of the Old Testament* (Chicago: Moody Press, 1999), 366.

sexual immorality and having gone after other flesh,[78] are exhibited as an example in undergoing the punishment of eternal fire." (Jude 7) On this, one liberal online group tries to justify Jude 7 this way,

> A likely interpretation is that the author of Jude criticized the men of Sodom for wanting to engage in sexual activities with angels. Angels are described in the Bible as a species of created beings who were different from humans. The sin of the people of Sodom would be that of bestiality. Another possibility is that the "*other flesh*" refers to cannibalism, which was a practice associated with early Canaanite culture. However, there is no mention in Genesis 19 about actually eating the angels.[79]

The Greek word *sarkos heteras* literally *went after different or other flesh*. First, we should mention that Jude focuses not on the attempted homosexual rape but rather the men of Sodom were desiring to engage in sexual relations with other men, same-sex relations, which he states was deserving of God's judgment. Second, it does no good to argue that these were angels, suggesting that this is why it refers to *different* or *other flesh*. The angels had materialized as men, looking no different from any other man, so the men of Sodom knew no different. The *Greek-English Lexicon of the New Testament* gives the meaning of *sarkos heteras* as, "ἀπέρχομαι ὀπίσω σαρκὸς ἑτέρας: (an idiom, literally 'to go after strange flesh') to engage in unnatural sexual intercourse—'to have homosexual intercourse.' ὡς Σόδομα καὶ Γόμορρα ... ἀπελθοῦσαι ὀπίσω σαρκὸς ἑτέρας 'they committed homosexual intercourse ... like the people of Sodom and Gomorrah' Jd 7. Though in some societies homosexuality is extremely rare, there are always ways of talking about it, though frequently the expressions may seem to be quite vulgar."[80] Thomas R. Schreiner wrote,

> Was Jude saying that Sodom was like the angels in Gen 6:1–4 in the sense that they also wanted sexual relations with angels?[81] If so, the sin criticized was not necessarily homosexuality but the violation of the separation established between human beings and angels. It is unlikely, however, that Jude made this specific point. The sin of Sodom was not precisely like the sin the angels committed. The most important evidence against the proposed

---

[78] Gr *sarkos heteras*; Lit *went after different or other flesh*; i.e., pursued unnatural fleshly desires

[79] What was the sin or sins of Sodom and Gomorrah?, http://www.religioustolerance.org/hombibg193.htm (accessed April 19, 2016).

[80] Johannes P. Louw and Eugene Albert Nida, *Greek-English Lexicon of the New Testament: Based on Semantic Domains* (New York: United Bible Societies, 1996), 771.

[81] For this view see Kelly, *Peter and Jude*, 258–59; Bauckham, *Jude, 2 Peter*, 54.

interpretation is that the men in Sodom who had a sexual desire for the angels *did not know they were angels.*[82] Their sin consisted in their homosexual intentions and their brutal disregard for the rights of visitors to the city.[83] Furthermore, it would be strange to designate a desire for angels as a desire for "other flesh" (*sarkos heteras*). The term more naturally refers to a desire for those of the same sex; they desired flesh other than that of women. For various reasons some are attempting today to question the view that homosexuality receives an unqualified negative verdict in the Scriptures. Such attempts have been singularly unsuccessful. The biblical writers and the Jewish tradition unanimously condemned homosexuality as evil.[84] The reason Jude introduced the example of Sodom and Gomorrah is that their punishment functions as an "example" (*deigma*) of what God will do to the opponents in the future.[85]

On this verse Max Anders in the *Holman New Testament Commentary* writes,

Not only ought we not to do the same sins as those who are disobedient, but we should try to expose them. Paul may be referring to exposing the sins of church members, because the church is responsible to hold its members accountable for their lifestyles. If a Christian lives in flagrant, unrepentant sin, the church is to try to get them to turn from their sin (Matt. 18:15–20; Gal. 6:1).

The context is dealing with the disobedient. This would indicate that the church should attempt to expose the sins of the non-Christian, which would be a full-time job if done very thoroughly. Society's major sins certainly need to be exposed.

Sins are exposed by shining light into sin's darkness. An amazing thing happens. Darkness can no longer hide its nature and acts in secret. All is exposed to light. Light that **makes everything visible** brings an even more radical element. Literally, this reads,

---

[82] Rightly Moo, *2 Peter, Jude*, 242.

[83] Contra D. G. Horrell, *The Epistles of Peter and Jude*, EC (Peterborough: Epworth, 1998), 121.

[84] For further discussion of this point see T. R. Schreiner, *Romans*, BECNT (Grand Rapids: Baker, 1998), 93–97. See also Oecumenius in *James, 1–2 Peter, 1–3 John, Jude*, ACCS (Downers Grove: InterVarsity, 2000), 251. For a full treatment of the issue of homosexuality, see now R. A. J. Gagnon, *The Bible and Homosexual Practice: Texts and Hermeneutics* (Nashville: Abingdon, 2001).

[85] Thomas R. Schreiner, *1, 2 Peter, Jude*, vol. 37, The New American Commentary (Nashville: Broadman & Holman Publishers, 2003), 452–453.

everything that is revealed is (or becomes) light. Light turns darkness into light. This is the church's mission. Whether the people in darkness are church members or society members, the goal is to transform them completely from darkness to light.

The poetic passage in verse 14 may be a quote from an ancient hymn based on Scripture. It is not a direct scriptural quotation. A person who was participating in the **deeds of darkness** is to wake up and **rise from the dead**, meaning to turn from those deeds. **Christ will shine on you** may mean that Christ is pleased with the person who turns from such deeds. He is light and the source of their light. His shining light exposes all their darkness and transforms them into light.[86]

Put to Death What Is Earthly in You

Colossians 3:5 Updated American Standard Version (UASV)

5 Therefore, Put to death therefore what is earthly in you: sexual immorality, impurity, passion, evil desire, and covetousness, which is idolatry.

One of the greatest mistakes of the Christian and religious leadership is, to be self-righteous in their dealings with those who have same-sex attraction, or those that have given into a homosexual lifestyle. The conduct of such ones is n more grievous that the spouse who commits adultery, or the churchgoer who commits fornication, or the churchgoer that finds himself or herself involved in the habit of masturbation or pornography. Sexual sin is sexual sin. There were Christians in the first century who had formerly led a life of homosexuality, who put on the new person as they worked toward becoming a Christian, getting control over themselves, and setting aside their former ways. — 1 Corinthians 6:9-11

Does God have the right to set the moral standards of humankind? Yes, he is the Creator of heaven and earth, as well as humans. He designed us to be free moral agents but under the umbrella of his sovereignty. We were never intended to have absolute freedom, the ability to set our own standards of right and wrong. Moreover, the natural desire is opposite sex attraction. The only reason that same-sex attraction exists at present is our fall into imperfection. It is a symptom of inherited imperfection. Once God has settled the issues raised by Satan and man's rebellion, we will no longer lean toward bad, but will lean toward good. The natural desire for Adam and Eve before the fall was toward good, and to think of or do bad would have been

---

[86] Max Anders, *Galatians-Colossians*, vol. 8, Holman New Testament Commentary (Nashville, TN: Broadman & Holman Publishers, 1999), 171.

contrary to that nature. After the rebellion and imperfection entered the world, the further removed humans were from Adam and Eve, the more they were and are inclined toward their imperfections, leaning toward bad.

How do we benefit from fighting the desires of the flesh, and obeying God's moral standards, as set out in Scripture? While it may seem unfair now that one cannot act on, nor entertain same-sex attraction, even though it may seem natural to him or her, this is a temporary situation. A time is coming when those, who have sided with God and have remained loyal, will receive eternal life. Can you imagine living for hundreds of millions of years, and looking back on that mere 70-80 years of imperfect desires?—John 3:16

God's View Homosexuality

While the liberal religious leaders of the day have watered down the Bible, this does not remove the clear statements from scripture. God created Adam and Eve, man and woman, with the desire, the sexual attraction of man toward woman and woman toward man. God is deeply saddened over the rebellion of Adam and Eve, and the subsequent fall into a sinful, depraved world. However, he is correcting the issues that were raised. God condemns all sin; that is all that is anything not in harmony with his personality, standards, ways, will, and purpose.[87]

What if you find yourself having feelings of same-sex attraction, does this necessarily mean that you are a homosexual, in the sense that you are not attracted, nor ever will be attracted to the same sex, and that you will fall away into having a sexual relationship with a person of the same sex. No. We do not fully understand our imperfections, and it could be a period of time that you feel this way. However, there is no sense in deceiving ourselves; some will only ever have a same-sex attraction in this imperfect age that we live in, and they are obligated to have control over themselves, just as the same as any other with inappropriate sexual desires. If one seeks out excellent, competent Christian counseling, can they put on the new person and take off the old person, to the point that they find themselves attracted to the opposite sex? Yes, some will be able to, but a few will have to live with and maintain control over their same-sex attraction until God brings this imperfect system of things to an end.

Just as some mental health professionals, believe that same-sex attraction is genetic, and others that it is social, they also believe the same thing about addictive personalities. They also believe the same thing about

---

[87] (See Job 2:10; Psa. 39:1; Lev. 20:20; 2 Cor. 12:21; Pro 21:4; Rom. 3:9-18; 2 Pet. 2:12-15; Heb. 3:12, 13, 18, 19)

adults that are sexually attracted to children. We have already agreed in the above that it is likely that it is both. You have a child who grows up in a household where he is sexually abused, and once he is older, the doctors diagnose him as having sexual attractions toward very young children. Now, just because this one has genetic leanings in the direction of young children, and he was socialized in this direction, there is no rational person who would make the argument, "this is who he is, God made him this way, he should be allowed to continue having sexual relations with children." Just because he was born with this leaning and was raised in such an environment that only perpetuated his desires, rational society would expect him to seek professional help. They would expect that he overcome his leanings, and if not, possibly acquire coping skills to maintain control. If he acts out, he would be arrested and locked away. While society has legalized or, at least, ignored the laws against homosexuality, God has not, and he expects that one get help to overcome, or gain control of the unnatural desires.

Aside from getting professional help from a Christian counselor, what can you do to gain control over your unnatural desires? You can pray to God, really going at him with the issues, opening your heart to him.

Psalm 139:23-24 Updated American Standard Version (UASV)

[23] Search me, O God, and know my heart;
  Examine me, and know my anxious[88] thoughts;
[24] And see whether there is in me any painful way,[89]
  And lead me in the everlasting way

Proverbs 23:7 says, "For as he thinks in his heart, so is he." If we are to get control over our irrational thinking, we do well to fill our mind with good thoughts. (Phil 4:8) This means that we need to be in God's Words daily. The Bible has the power to mold our mind. (Heb. 4:12) Scripture can have a powerful effect on our thinking if we study it in the appropriate way.

Another measure that needs to be taken is the fleeing from anything that will generate wrong desires, which lead to wrong actions. This means keeping our eyes and ears away from pornography and homosexual advocates. (Col. 3:5) We need to understand that the Bible's moral values are not respected in today's world.

Parents, teachers, coaches and the like influenced the youth of the 1950s and 1960s. Most young people today are very much influenced by hip-hop, rap, and heavy metal music, as well reality television, celebrities, movies,

---

[88] Or *disquieting*

[89] Or *hurtful way*

video games, and the internet, especially social media. Parents are now allowing their children to receive life-altering opinions, beliefs, and worldviews from the likes of Snooki, a cast member of the MTV reality show *Jersey Shore*. Kim Kardashian and her family rose to prominence with their reality television series, *Keeping Up with the Kardashians*.

The ABC Family Channel (owned by Disney) comes across as a channel that you would want you children watching. However, most of the shows are nothing more than dysfunctional families, promotions of homosexuality as an alternative lifestyle, and young actors and actresses that are playing underage teens in high school, running around killing, causing havoc, and having sexual intercourse with multiple characters on the show. In August 2006, an all-new slogan and visual style premiered on ABC Family: A New Kind of Family. The channel shows such programming as Pretty Little Liars, Twisted, The Fosters, Melissa & Joey, Switched at Birth, The Lying Game, Bunheads and Baby Daddy.

The world has added new words to their vocabulary, like "sexting," which is the act of sending sexually explicit messages and/or photographs, primarily between cell phones. The term was first popularized in 2007. Then, there is "F-Bomb," which we are not going to define fully other than to say that the dictionary considers it "a lighthearted and printable euphemism" for something far more offensive. If all of the above is unfamiliar to us as parents, and we have a teen or preteen child, we may want to Google the information.

Regardless of the degree of the relationship, these relationships often influence the thinking of a young life. It is important that we do not allow the wrong persons to change our children or us. The truth is our thoughts, and our actions are a direct result of bad associations, be it the bad friends, music, celebrities, video games, or social media. The same holds true of good relationships, like our parents, teachers, coaches, and good friends. Paul warned, "For there are many **rebellious men**, **empty talkers**, and **deceivers**," from whom we should watch out! – Titus 1:10.

In the end, with help from God's Word, the Christian congregation, the pastor, family, and Christian counseling, you have a reasonable expectation that you will not act on the same-sex desires. Moreover, there is the possibility that you may be one of the few that begins to alter oneself to the point that the desires are no more. If not, self-control will be the way of things until God brings this wicked age to an end. The final warning offered herein is this. Do not allow charismatic religious rhetoric to suggest that you can be healed by laying on of hands. This will only leave you vulnerable, as you will then let down your guard, and not seek the help that you need. What they espouse is just not how it works and is unbiblical.

CHAPTER 3 Explaining the Bible's View of Homosexuality

'If I was lying on my deathbed and I had kept this secret and never ever did anything about it, I would be lying there saying, "You just blew your entire life. You never dealt with yourself," and I don't want that to happen,' Bruce Jenner said in her Vanity Fair interview, who is now known as "Caitlyn Jenner."

Miley Cyrus came out as a pansexual (i.e., a sexuality that expresses itself in many different forms), saying, 'I am literally open to every single thing that is consenting and doesn't involve an animal, and everyone is of age,' she told Paper magazine. 'Everything that's legal, I'm down with. Yo, I'm down with any adult — anyone over the age of 18 who is down to love me. I don't relate to being boy or girl, and I don't have to have my partner relate to boy or girl.'

There is actually a coming out day, 11 October. On this day, in an article in Gay Star News, **22 celebrities who came out and changed the world in 2015**, *Roger Rock*, a retired British rail worker comments, "Congratulations to all of you - well done I wish I'd come out a lot earlier than 54 it will 20 years next year - never looked back!" From Toronto, Ontario, who studied at the University of Toronto, Paula Key commented on the same above article. "So happy to blog these lesbians on … There is such a need for gays/lesbians in homophobic countries to learn about their history. Just over 200, 212 visitors - the need is there."[90]

The Advocate is an American LGBT-interest magazine, printed bi-monthly, ran an article, 53 People Who Came Out This Year, referring to 2015. They write, "We're always glad when anyone comes out, although it's particularly noteworthy when well-known people do. They provide role models for young LGBT people and drive home the message that we are everywhere while usually enhancing their own lives in the process — living openly and honestly is good for the soul. We're looking back at some famous folks who've come out as lesbian, gay, bisexual, transgender, pansexual, or fluid this year. Of course, you don't have to be famous for your coming-out to make an impact. When people know someone who is LGBT, they're far more likely to support our rights. 'Every person who speaks up changes more

---

[90] 22 celebrities who came out and made 2015 the best year ..,

http://www.gaystarnews.com/article/25-celebrities-who-made-2015-the-best-year-ev (accessed April 23, 2016).

hearts and minds, and creates new advocates for equality,' notes the Human Rights Campaign."[91]

Pew Research Center[92]

Acceptance of homosexuality is rising across the broad spectrum of American Christianity, including among members of churches that strongly oppose homosexual relationships as sinful, according to an extensive Pew Research Center survey of U.S. religious beliefs and practices.

Amid a changing religious landscape that has seen a declining percentage of Americans who identify as Christian, a majority of U.S. Christians (54%) now say that homosexuality should be accepted, rather than discouraged, by society. While this is still considerably lower than the shares of religiously unaffiliated people (83%) and members of non-Christian faiths (76%) who say the same, the Christian figure has increased by 10 percentage points since we conducted a similar study in 2007. It reflects a growing acceptance of homosexuality among all Americans – from 50% to 62% – during the same period.

Among Christians, this trend is driven partly by younger church members, who are generally more accepting of homosexuality than their elder counterparts. For example, roughly half (51%) of evangelical Protestants in the Millennial generation (born between 1981 and 1996) say homosexuality should be accepted by society, compared with a third of evangelical Baby Boomers and a fifth of evangelicals in the Silent generation. Generational differences with similar patterns also are evident among Catholics, mainline Protestants and members of the historically black Protestant tradition.

At the same time, however, a larger segment of older adults in some Christian traditions have become accepting of homosexuality in recent years, helping to drive the broader trend. For instance, 32% of evangelical

---

[91] 53 People Who Came Out This Year | Advocate.com,

http://www.advocate.com/people/2015/12/23/53-people-who-came-out-year (accessed April 23, 2016).

[92] The Pew Research Center is a nonpartisan American think tank which is based in Washington, D.C. It provides information on social issues, public opinion, and demographic trends shaping the United States and the world. It also conducts public opinion polling, demographic research, media content analysis, and other empirical social science research. Pew Research Center does not take explicit policy positions and is a subsidiary of The Pew Charitable Trusts. – Pew Research Center - Wikipedia, the free encyclopedia, https://en.wikipedia.org/wiki/Pew_Research_Center (accessed April 23, 2016).

Protestant Baby Boomers now say homosexuality should be accepted, up from 25% in 2007.

Regardless of age, seven-in-ten Catholics – whose church teaches that homosexual behavior is "intrinsically disordered" – say that homosexuality should be accepted by society, a 12-percentage-point increase since 2007. Similar jumps have occurred among mainline Protestants (from 56% to 66%), Orthodox Christians (from 48% to 62%) and members of the historically black Protestant tradition (from 39% to 51%).

Most Mormons and evangelical Protestants still say homosexuality should be discouraged by society – in line with the teachings of many of their churches – but 36% of both groups say it should be accepted. Among Mormons, there was a 12-point increase (from 24% to 36%) in acceptance since 2007, and among evangelicals there was a 10-point rise (from 26% to 36%). Jehovah's Witnesses remain perhaps the most opposed of any U.S religious tradition toward homosexuality, with just 16% saying it should be accepted by society.

The trend of growing acceptance is evident across many specific Protestant denominations, including some conservative denominations with official teachings that remain strongly opposed to same-sex marriage. For example, among members of the Lutheran Church-Missouri Synod, the share saying homosexuality should be accepted by society grew by 12 points (from 44% to 56%) between 2007 and 2014. And although Pentecostals who identify with the Assemblies of God remain largely opposed to homosexuality, 26% now say it should be accepted by society, up from 16% in 2007.

Among members of the Southern Baptist Convention – an evangelical church and the nation's largest Protestant denomination – the share saying homosexuality should be accepted increased 7 points, from 23% to 30%.

Members of several mainline churches – some of which have officially embraced same-sex marriage – have become even more accepting of homosexuality in recent years. For instance, 73% of members of the Evangelical Lutheran Church in America now say it should be accepted by society, up from 56% in 2007. Members of the United Methodist Church, the Episcopal Church, the Presbyterian Church (U.S.A.) and the United Church of Christ also have become more accepting toward homosexuality.[93]

---

[93] More U.S. Christians OK with ... - Pew Research Center, http://www.pewresearch.org/fact-tank/2015/12/18/most-u-s-christian-groups-grow-m (accessed April 23, 2016).

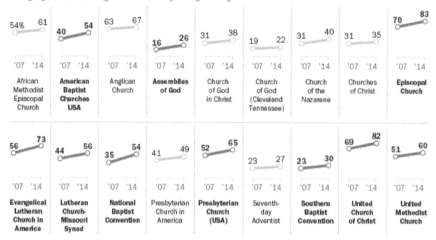

Members of many Protestant denominations now more accepting of homosexuality

% saying homosexuality should be accepted by society

'07 '14	'07 '14	'07 '14	'07 '14	'07 '14	'07 '14	'07 '14	'07 '14	'07 '14
54% 61	40 54	63 67	16 26	31 38	19 22	31 40	31 35	70 83
African Methodist Episcopal Church	American Baptist Churches USA	Anglican Church	Assemblies of God	Church of God in Christ	Church of God (Cleveland Tennessee)	Church of the Nazarene	Churches of Christ	Episcopal Church

'07 '14	'07 '14	'07 '14	'07 '14	'07 '14	'07 '14	'07 '14	'07 '14	'07 '14
56 73	44 56	35 54	41 49	52 65	23 27	23 30	69 82	51 60
Evangelical Lutheran Church in America	Lutheran Church-Missouri Synod	National Baptist Convention	Presbyterian Church in America	Presbyterian Church (USA)	Seventh-day Adventist	Southern Baptist Convention	United Church of Christ	United Methodist Church

Source: 2014 Religious Landscape Study, conducted June 4-Sept. 30, 2014. Statistically significant change shown in bold.

PEW RESEARCH CENTER

TheRichest.com claims to be "the world's leading source of shocking and intriguing content surrounding celebrities, money, global events, society, pop culture, sports, and much more." They write, "The year was 2003, Britney shocked the world when she and Madonna went into a kiss with full-on mouth-to-mouth. After the fact, Spears announced that she had never kissed a female before and never would again. In an interview with CNN, the pop star stated, 'I didn't know it was going to be that long and everything.' Evidently, she and Madonna discussed the possibility during rehearsals but did not have a solid plan. When asked if she would 'do it again,' she decided that she would not, but maybe if it was Madonna again."[94]

The world is going liberal-progressive right before our eyes. The above, while once shocking, is a regular occurrence. There are more websites than can be counted that run articles about homosexuals and homosexuality. The comments on these innumerable sites are into the millions likely. If one takes a stand as a Christian, saying homosexuality is a sin, they are labeled a homophobe, a bigot, prejudiced and judgmental. Many are afraid to defend the Word of God and their faith.

We must understand that just as this generation is rapidly growing to accept homosexuality as an alternative lifestyle, the same is true of many

---

[94] 10 Shocking Same Sex Celebrity Kisses - TheRichest, http://www.therichest.com/rich-list/most-shocking/10-shocking-same-sex-celebrity (accessed April 23, 2016).

Christian beliefs. However, God's Word is true, and the values, morals, and ethics therein are always the same and do not change because of public opinion.

Ephesians 4:14 Updated American Standard Version (UASV)

[14] So that we may no longer be children, tossed to and fro by the waves and carried about by every wind of teaching, by the trickery of men, by craftiness with regard to the scheming of deceit;

On this verse, Max Anders writes, "The Ephesian church, as most of the churches Paul wrote, faced teachers with opposing viewpoints. They divided the church body into factions, each opposing the others. Their presence required the type of spiritual maturity and church unity Paul had described. Without such unity the church would act like a group of babies, each crying out because of his own pains and needs, each inconsistently saying one thing and then another, each at the mercy of cunning, deceitful teachers. To avoid infantile behavior, the church must mature into unity of the faith and of knowledge of Christ."[95]

When it comes to Satan's world, which Jesus said we were to be no part of (John 15:19; 17:14-16), and Paul said that while we must live in the world, we need not fully use it. (1 Cor. 7:31) What did Paul mean? "To handle matters of this life properly, Christians must remember that these things are not permanent. On the one hand, believers live in this world with its pleasure, pain, and responsibilities. On the other hand, they belong to the next world that will replace this life forever. This is why Paul described his own life in paradoxical terms: dying but living, beaten but not killed, sorrowful but rejoicing, poor but making others rich, having nothing but owning everything (2 Cor. 6:9–10).[96]

On the subject of homosexuality, true Christians adhere to the Bible's view. What is the Bible's view of homosexuality? If we are to obey the Bible and not water down the Word of God, how are we to evangelize those who see us as a homophobe, a bigot, prejudiced and judgmental?

What is the Bible's View of Homosexuality?

We have covered this extensively in chapters 1 and 2, so we will only offer the gist here. We were created in the image of God, and we were

---

[95] Max Anders, *Galatians-Colossians*, vol. 8, Holman New Testament Commentary (Nashville, TN: Broadman & Holman Publishers, 1999), 153.

[96] Richard L. Pratt Jr, *I & II Corinthians*, vol. 7, Holman New Testament Commentary (Nashville, TN: Broadman & Holman Publishers, 2000), 121–122.

designed male and female, to have sexual relations between one man and one woman, only within the marriage arrangement. Men are not to have sexual relations with a male, as with a woman, nor are women to have sexual relations with a woman as with a man; it is an abomination. (Gen. 1:27-28; Lev. 18:22; Pro 5:18-19) The Bible condemns fornication (Gr. *Porneia*, sexual immorality), which applies to both homosexual and forbidden heterosexual conduct." (Gal. 5:19-21) Sexual immorality unlawful sexual intercourse includes adultery, prostitution, sexual relations between unmarried individuals, homosexuality, and bestiality.

How Should Christians View Homosexuality?

We do not hate homosexuals. Nevertheless, we cannot approve of same-sex relationships of any kind. We can empathize with those who struggle with same-sex attractions, as many heterosexuals struggle with inappropriate sexual attractions to persons of the opposite sex that they ought not. We proudly but not arrogantly live by the moral code found within the Bible. This is our lifestyle choice, just as some have made homosexuality their lifestyle choice. We will not hate those who are free to make choices at odds with ours, even if many evidence hatred of us, viewing us as a homophobe, a bigot, prejudiced and judgmental. We will not be ashamed of what we have a right to, a biblical worldview. — Joshua 24:15; Psalm 119:46.

Are Christians to Respect Everyone?

"Unquestionably, the Bible says: "Honor **all people**, love the brotherhood, fear God, honor the king." or, "**Respect everyone**, love other believers, honor God, and respect the Emperor." (1 Pet 2:17, NASB and GNT) However, we have a problem with the word homophobic, as it is defined as "showing an irrational hatred, **disapproval**, or fear of homosexuality, gay and lesbian people, or their culture." (Bold mine) If anyone asks us if we are homophobic, we will have to qualify it. Why? If we just say that we are not homophobic, they might believe we **do not** disapprove of it.

Are you homophobic? Respond, "I do not have any hatred of homosexuals, or fear of homosexuality, gay and lesbian people, or their culture. However, I do not approve of same-sex relations of any kind, except friendships."

Is the Christian Stance Not Encouraging Prejudice Against Homosexuals?

Certainly not, Christians reject homosexual relations, not the people themselves. If any Christian do otherwise, they are not being obedient to God's Word. True Christians cannot be faulted for radical Christian groups like the Westboro Baptist Church, who are nothing more than hate mongers. If we look at the link to their homepage (http://www.godhatesfags.com/), we can see that they are not true Christians. They and a handful of other groups like them are but a few thousand at most out of 200 countries with more than 2.18 billion Christians. Of course, not all of these 5.18 billion make up genuine Christianity. Indeed, there are those within the LBGT community who would say that others are radical and hate Christians merely because they are Christians. We as Christians cannot fault the whole for the select few. We are not to be prejudiced toward the LBGT community and hope that they will not be prejudiced toward us. We both can respect each other as persons and agree to disagree on some issues.

Did Jesus Teach Tolerance?

First, let us define "tolerance." Like any word, it has different meanings in different contexts. It can mean **(1)** acceptance of different views, **(2)** putting up with somebody or something irritating or otherwise unpleasant, **(3)** ability to endure hardship, and **(4)** the loss of effect that a drug can have. Our meaning is number **(1)**, which can be better defined as "the acceptance of the differing views of other people, e.g., in religious or political matters, and fairness toward the people who hold these different views."

Second, let us take a brief look at Jesus. While Christians indeed seek to imitate him to the best of their ability, it is impossible to do so entirely, as we are imperfect, while he was a perfect man, as well as divine, the Son of God. In addition, he is the judge of whether someone receives eternal life or eternal destruction. (Matt. 25:31-46; 2 Thess. 1:8) Therefore, Jesus can judge a person as to life or death, for he can read hearts and minds. Humans are not to judge in this sense, nor do they have those abilities.

Third, Jesus did not have tolerance, accepting different views, as he clearly stated, "My food is to do the will of him [the Father] who sent me and to accomplish his work." (John 4:34) He also said, "Truly, truly, I say to you; the Son can do nothing of his own accord, but only what he sees the Father doing. For whatever the Father does, that the Son does likewise ... I can do nothing on my own. As I hear, I judge, and my judgment is just because I seek not my own will but the will of him who sent me." (John 5:19, 30) Jesus' will would be the same as the Father's will and vice versa. They are one, in full agreement, and there are no divisions between them, as they are united in the same mind and the same judgment. Christians seek to be one as they are one. – John 10:30.

We can understand the values, the character, the moral code of the Father and the Son because of Scriptural revelation. Jesus would not accept any view that was not in harmony with his and the Father's personality, standards, ways, and will. (Lev. 20:20; Num. 9:13; Job 2:10; Ps 39:1; 2 Cor. 12:21; Jam. 4:17) Christians with a biblical worldview would agree, be united in the same mind and with the same purpose. Therefore, no, Jesus would not tolerate homosexuality, and nor would Christians. Any congregation that would allow a homosexual to become a member of that congregation, let alone a pastor or bishop, would be contrary to the above and the rest of the Scriptures. They would be false teachers, leading people astray. They are 'untaught and unstable as they distort Paul's teachings, as they also do the rest of the Scriptures, to their own destruction.' (2 Pet. 3:16) Just because Christians do not tolerate or accept different views that are in conflict with Scripture (e.g., homosexuality), this does not mean that they are to disrespect such ones.

Is Not Homosexuality Genetically Predisposed?

The Bible does not directly disclose that same-sex attraction is genetic. However, it could be inferred from God's curse of Canaan (the forefather of the Canaanites), the grandson of Noah, who, it appears, sexually assaulted Noah when he was unconscious from alcohol. It can be inferred that we inherit leanings and dispositions. Certainly, we inherit sin, i.e., imperfection. (Rom. 5:12) In addition, the Bible does say that some of our imperfect traits are deeply ingrained. (2 Cor. 10:4-5) Therefore, if homosexuality is predisposed to some, this does not equate that "God made me this way." It only means it is imperfection passed on like any other. Thus, the fault lies with Satan and Adam.

Many accept that anger can have a genetic root. If this is true and at present, there is no reason to doubt it, are we to accept men beating their wives or wives beating their children because they may have been genetically predisposed to anger? Science argues that pedophilia is a genetic predisposition, so are we to claim that pedophiles are acceptable? Some claim that alcoholism is genetic, so do we accept alcoholics as a part of the norm? Some from the LGBT community are offended when pedophiles are brought into the conversation because those sexual acts are an abomination, disgusting, revolting, and rightly, they do not want to be associated with such

67

ones. However, God feels the same way about homosexuality. We would expect those with anger issues, those suffering from alcoholism, and those preferring child-sex (pedophile) would get control over themselves and avoid such unsavory activity. God's Word expects the same from those who have same-sex attraction.

Is It Not Cruel to Tell Those with Same-Sex Attraction to Control Themselves?

We would not accept a pedophile just because they have a child-sex attraction. Yes, God gave us sexual impulses, natural desires. However, sin, i.e., imperfection, came into the world through Adam, and death through sin, imperfection, and so death spread to all men because all sinned, i.e., are imperfect. (Rom 5:1) We expect people that have impulses for things we find revolting not to act on them but tend to rationalize when our impulses are pointed out. Christian 'Therefore consider the members of their earthly body as dead to immorality, impurity, passion, evil desire, and greed, which amounts to idolatry.' – Colossians 3:5.

The LGBT community and all others live by some ethical code, which means that there are things that they view as deplorable. They would agree that stealing is terrible and unacceptable. The Bible and thus Christians with a biblical worldview have a moral code, which prohibits certain behaviors and certain types of sexual conduct, e.g., homosexuality. (1 Cor. 6:9-10) The Bible is not unreasonable, nor is it encouraging its readers to be prejudiced. The Bible expects those with same-sex attraction to do the same as those with an opposite-sex attraction, namely, "Flee from sexual immorality!" (1 Cor. 6:18) The Greek word *porneia* (sexual immorality) includes unlawful sexual intercourse, namely, adultery, prostitution, sex between unmarried individuals, homosexuality, and bestiality. Many do not realize that there are millions of *heterosexuals* trying to get control over their sexually immoral leanings as well. If a person with same-sex attraction wants to conform to the Word of God, they can live happily without fulfilling their sexual urges. If their desire to please God is greater, this can be the case. Remember, it is only temporary.

We should shun experimenting with conduct that the Bible describes as sexually immoral if we want to please God. (Eph. 4:19; 5:11) Over the last few decades, it has been socialized for boys to see lesbians as sexually appealing but gay men as unappealing. Almost all movies, TV, and music today promote girls kissing girls. In the last few years, they have started promoting guys kissing guys. One cultural difference should make the point. In the 1980s, a teen couple might be caught kissing behind the bleachers at a basketball or football game by a teacher. Today, it is an entirely different situation. The modern-day junior high school children (13 and 14 years old); literally view oral sex as being no different than kissing one another on the lips. According to one survey, about 50% of all teens (15 to 19) have engaged in oral sex. Teens today do not think that oral sex is that big of a deal!

The thinking of the teen girls is that they cannot get pregnant but can please their boyfriend by performing oral sex. They do not see oral sex as sex. That is why they see oral sex as harmless. However, there are health risks to oral sex. They can contract hepatitis (A or B), genital warts, gonorrhea, herpes, HIV, and syphilis. Any conduct involving the genitals of another person, which would include intercourse, oral sex, anal sex, and masturbating another person, is sex. Denying something is something does not change what it is.

Oral sex can have harmful physical, emotional, and mental consequences, taking a toll on you. The young on having or performing oral sex can feel just as used, regretful, and vulnerable as any teen having vaginal sex. The same bad emotions that you might experience from having intercourse in the wrong set of circumstances can result from oral sex as well.

Sex can refer to such things as oral sex, anal sex, or masturbating another person. The truth is you have engaged in any of these forms of sex, you are no longer a virgin.

When we think of ethics, morality, and the conscience, teens tend to drown that conversation out. However, let us touch on it briefly. **Ethics** is moral principles that govern a person's behavior or the conducting of an activity. **Morality** is principles concerning the distinction between right and wrong or good and bad behavior. The **conscience** is an internal compass inside of every human that enables him or her to determine between right and wrong. These are not religious terms alone. Even atheists have ethical values, moral principles, and a conscience. As an illustration, think of the traffic laws in your city. Are they a restriction to your freedom, or are they protecting? Yes, traffic laws indeed restrict your absolute freedom, but they also protect society from themselves and others. What has happened to many teens that have ignored the laws about texting and driving? Having good ethical values, moral principles, and conscience may seem restrictive, but they also help you protect your life and well-being. If you ignore them, you will certainly suffer the consequences of your own actions.

Galatians 6:7 Updated American Standard Version (UASV)

7 Do not be deceived: God is not to be mocked, for whatever a person sows, this he will also reap.

To support his admonition to give, Paul shares a principle of cause and effect. A grave warning states that **God cannot be mocked**. Why? Because a man **reaps what he sows**. *Mocked* means "to turn up one's nose" or "treat with contempt." One who turns up his nose at God and sneers at him doesn't change this immutable "law of the harvest." Disregarding God's counsel, we will always suffer. Each of us by our thoughts, attitudes, and actions is constantly planting for a future reaping. Time may pass before the crop ripens, but the harvest is inevitable. Consider the harvest! In this application of the harvest principle, by giving (sowing) to our spiritual leaders, we can expect to reap a spiritual harvest of abundant ministry. In contrast, a Christian who fails to support his spiritual leaders is sneering at God and can expect discipline. Such a selfish Christian spends his resources to gratify his own personal desires. In contrast, the Christian who shares his finances adds interest to the capital of **eternal life**. In a broader application of this principle, remember there are no miracle crops. You reap spiritually, relationally, mentally, and physically in direct relation to what you plant. It is foolish to think that you can live irresponsibly and not suffer damaging consequences. Yet to the generous, Paul shares an encouraging promise: **Let us not become weary in doing good, for at the proper time we will reap a harvest if we do not give up**. It is discouraging to continue to do good and not see a reward. Paul challenges the Galatians to keep on giving because God promises to reward those who are faithful in the long run.[97]

1 Peter 3:16 Updated American Standard Version (UASV)

[16] having a good conscience, so that, when you are slandered, those who revile your good behavior in Christ may be put to shame.

If we maintain our testimony with gentleness and respect, we can be confident of operating with a **clear conscience.** This means that we should live in such a way that we won't have to keep looking over our shoulder, hoping that the wrong we have done isn't about to catch up to us.

By operating this way, our behavior and words will speak volumes to those who come against us. Peter promised that truth will prevail. What is not clear is whether the reference to the slanderers being ashamed refers to their present life or to the future

---

[97] Max Anders, *Galatians-Colossians*, vol. 8, Holman New Testament Commentary (Nashville, TN: Broadman & Holman Publishers, 1999), 79–80.

day of God's judgment. Most likely the text looks to a change of heart by the persecutors in this life as they are confronted by the gracious responses of the people they are persecuting.[98]

Colossians 3:5 Updated American Standard Version (UASV)

⁵ Deaden, therefore, your members on the earth: sexual immorality,[99] uncleanness, passion, **evil desire**, and greediness, which is idolatry.

Evil Desire, lust, coveting, craving: (Gr. *epithymia*) This is an inordinate, self-indulgent craving to have what belongs to another or engage in what is morally wrong, which displaces our affection for God.–Gal. 5:16; 1 Tim. 6:9; 2 Tim. 2:22; 1 Pet. 1:14)

Matthew 5:28 Updated American Standard Version (UASV)

²⁸ but I say to you that everyone who looks at a woman with **lust** for her has already committed adultery with her in his heart.

ἐπιθυμία [*epithumia*] is a strong desire to have what belongs to another, as well as becoming involved in anything that is morally wrong, i.e., coveting, lusting, evil desires, and the like.

Ephesians 5:3 Updated American Standard Version (UASV)

³ But **sexual immorality**, and all uncleanness, or greediness, must not even be named among you, as is proper among holy ones;

Sexual Immorality: (Heb. *zanah*; Gr. *porneia*) A general term for immoral sexual acts of any kind: such as adultery, prostitution, sexual relations between people not married to each other, homosexuality, and bestiality.– Num. 25:1; Deut. 22:21; Matt. 5:32; 1 Cor. 5:1.

Galatians 5:19-21 Updated American Standard Version (UASV)

¹⁹ Now the works of the flesh are evident, which are: **sexual immorality**, impurity, **sensuality**, ²⁰ idolatry, sorcery, enmity, strife, jealousy, fits of anger, rivalries, dissensions, divisions, ²¹ envy, drunkenness, orgies, and things like these. I warn you, as I warned you before, that those who do such things will not inherit the kingdom of God.

Sensuality, debauchery, licentiousness, lewdness: (Gr. *aselgeia*) This is being completely unrestrained in our moral attitudes and behaviors, with the inference of sexual licentiousness. This is one who indulges in

---

[98] David Walls and Max Anders, *I & II Peter, I, II & III John, Jude*, vol. 11, Holman New Testament Commentary (Nashville, TN: Broadman & Holman Publishers, 1999), 55.

[99] Gr *porneia*

sensual pleasure without any regard for morality. – Mark 7:22; Rom. 13:13; 2 Cor. 12:21; Gal. 5:19; Eph. 4:19; 1 Pet. 4:3; 2 Pet. 2:2, 7, 18; Jude 5-7.

The entertainment industry indoctrinated our young ones to not consider oral sex wrong, but rather no different from kissing. If we feed our minds on such things, it will only enhance the leanings we may already have. The Bible offers us eternal life, and it is an attainable goal for any of us if we choose not to act on any wrong desires.

CHAPTER 4 Avoiding Homosexuality and Controlling Same-Sex Attraction?

"I remember that once when I slept with a girlfriend, I had a strong desire to kiss her and that I did so. I could not help being terribly inquisitive over her body, for she had always kept it hidden from me. . . . I go into ecstasies every time I see the naked figure of a woman. . . . It strikes me as so wonderful and exquisite that I have difficulty in stopping the tears rolling down my cheeks. If only I had a girlfriend. – Anne Frank[100]

How many gay people are there in the United States? "The Williams Institute at the UCLA School of Law, a sexual orientation law and public policy think tank, estimates that 9 million (about 3.8%) of Americans identify as gay, lesbian, bisexual or transgender (2011). The institute also found that bisexuals make up 1.8% of the population while 1.7% are gay or lesbian. The number of LGBT persons in the U.S. is subjective. Studies pointing to the statistics are estimates at best. The most widely accepted statistic is that 1 in every 10 individuals is LGBT; however, some research estimates 1 in 20."[101] With the internet conversation being flooded with articles on homosexuality and inundated on discussion sites, one might think the statistic would be much higher. Homosexuality is talked about more openly today than it was several decades ago. One would have to be a very brave soul to say that they disapprove of such a lifestyle. The person would be labeled a homophobe, that they were prejudiced and judgmental. The scathing comments would be so overwhelming; it might be tempting to remain silent about one's position on this hot-button topic.

Yong Christians are afraid to take a stand for biblical truths. In addition, it has also created a permissive attitude that has popularized experimentation with same-sex relationships. Many young girls claim to be lesbian, bisexual, or bi-curious. Other young girls have propositioned female Christian girls as young as twelve. These are serious pressure moments because to reject such propositions can get one labeled a homophobe, a religious zealot. The new mentality of today is that homosexuality is just an alternative lifestyle. We have young ones who are attracted to the same-sex, who may be afraid to express their feelings to a pastor, who is not equipped to have such a

---

[100] She is one of the most discussed Jewish victims of the Holocaust. Her diary, The Diary of a Young Girl, which documents her life in hiding.

[101] Gay Population Statistics, http://gaylife.about.com/od/comingout/a/population.htm (accessed April 24, 2016).

conversation. They may feel that they are a homosexual and thus condemned for their feelings, which they have tried to shake but just will not go away.

What Causes Homosexuality

We will discuss whether we have a genetic predisposition in an upcoming chapter: Homosexuality – Genes or learned? For now, we must address some things that some of the LGBT community tries to deny. Over time, the things that we feed our minds on will play a role in same-sex attraction. Some men start watching porn that is between a man and a woman. Of course, after time, it is like drugs. He needs something more hardcore. Therefore, he moves on to lesbian porn. Then, he advances to shemale on shemale porn. A shemale is a transvestite, a passive male homosexual. Shemale is a term used in sex work to describe trans women with male genitalia and augmented female breasts from breast augmentation and/or hormones. In this, he convinces himself that he gets to watch what appear to be two women. After some time, the male genitalia now arouses him, so he is building himself up to same-sex attraction.

Another factor that contributes to homosexuality is abuse as a child. When a young child is forced or coerced into having sex with a parent or relative of the same sex, it lays the groundwork for same-sex attraction. Then, we couple this with the experiences that the young one goes through in grade school, junior high, and high school. Then, some young boys lack a father's sensitivity, so they seek to bond with other males. One of the problems that the church faces are, they do not address homosexuality, or when they do, it is a charismatic sermon, which hits heavily on the abhorrent factor. So much so that anyone struggling with same-sex attraction will only withdraw into themselves. Eventually, they will act on those desires. Then, there is the mistaken stereotype that homosexuals are sexual deviants or sexual predators. Therefore, those struggling with same-sex attraction feel like they are perverts, suffering great shame and excessive guilt, which means it is unlikely they will come forward seeking help. The goal of the church counsel is not to make someone straight but rather to help the person mature in Christ, put on the new person, and have the mind of Christ. Some are trading their unmet needs in same-sex feelings to get filled in their relationship with Christ.

God's View of Homosexuality

We have covered this extensively in earlier chapters, so we will only offer its gist here again. We were created in the image of God, and we were designed male and female to have sexual relations between one man and one woman, only within the marriage arrangement. Men are not to have sexual relations with a male, as with a woman, nor are women to have sexual relations with a woman as with a man; it is an abomination. (Gen. 1:27-28; Lev. 18:22; Pro 5:18-19) The Bible condemns fornication (Gr. *Porneia*, sexual immorality), which applies to both homosexual and forbidden heterosexual conduct." (Gal. 5:19-21) Sexual immorality unlawful sexual intercourse includes adultery, prostitution, sexual relations between unmarried individuals, homosexuality, and bestiality.

What about those who argue that God's Word was written some 2,000 – 3,500 ago, making it out of date? They make such an argument because their desires are greater than their knowledge of God's Word. They do not believe that it is fully inerrant and inspired but rather believe it is the word of man. They do not wish to face their desires, so they see anyone accepting the Bible as inspired and fully inerrant, as foolish. It teaches something different from what they want to believe and is at odds with their same-sex attraction. We do not want to be closed-minded in our thinking.

If one has same-sex attraction but does not act on those sexual leanings, the biblical truth is that this does not make them a homosexual. If you are young, and your passions are strong, easily sexually aroused, coupled with social pressure, same-sex attraction may be something that passes with time. Until this time has passed, you must refrain from homosexual practices of any sort. How?

Prayer: King David prayed, "Search me, O God, and know my heart! Try me and know my thoughts! And see if there be any grievous way in me, and lead me in the way everlasting!" (Ps 139:23-24) God by His Word can strengthen us, helping us to control our thoughts, as well as our desires. The apostle Paul encouraged us to, "In nothing be anxious; but in everything by prayer and supplication with thanksgiving let your requests be made known to God. And the peace of God, which surpasses all understanding, will guard your hearts and your minds[102] in Christ Jesus." (Phil. 4:6-7) Yes, if we can know that "the supreme power belongs to God, not to us." – 2 Corinthians 4:7.

Replace Bad Self-talk with Upbuilding Self-Talk: A daily Bible reading schedule is paramount. The apostle Paul said, "Finally, brothers, whatever is true, whatever is honorable, whatever is just, whatever is pure, whatever is lovely, whatever is of good report; if there be any virtue, and if there be any praise, **think on[103] these things**." (Phil 4:8) Paul also told us that "the word of God is living and active, sharper than any two-edged sword,

---

[102] Or "your mental powers; your thoughts."

[103] Or "dwell on these things; *ponder these things*"

75

piercing to the division of soul and of spirit, of joints and of marrow, and discerning the thoughts and intentions of the heart." – Hebrews 4:12.

The Pornography Trap: This will be dealt with more extensively in the chapter on Pornography. Nevertheless, it is best to read the basics here and then reread it yet again.

Pornography can fuel a same-sex attraction that may not even be established as genetic. If we are a young girl looking at images of naked women, or even sensually dressed women, with lustful intent in our hearts, how is this helping us to get control over ourselves? When God sees us looking at such material, is He not going to be devastatingly hurt, feel betrayed, and feel as though we have abandoned him? The information below is based on helping heterosexual couples but has been adapted to those struggling with same-sex attraction as well. This is not misinterpreting the Scriptures or twisting the Scriptures but instead taking the principles for heterosexuals and applying them to those who struggle with same-sex attraction.

Damage to Us Spiritually

Colossians 3:5 Updated American Standard Version (UASV)

⁵ Therefore, Put to death therefore what is earthly in you: sexual immorality, impurity, passion, evil desire, and covetousness, which is idolatry.

In telling believers to **put to death** certain behaviors, Paul is calling for complete extermination, not careful regulation. What must go? Paul gives us an "outside in" perspective. He starts with external actions and then moves to the internal drives which cause the conduct. In his "vice lists," Paul mentions three categories of behavior: (1) perverted passions, (2) hot tempers, (3) sharp tongues.

> First on the list is **sexual immorality** (*porneia*), a broad, general term for all kinds of illicit sexual behavior. God created sex to be enjoyed by one woman and one man in the confines of marriage. Any sexual activity that does not fit that definition is not to be part of a believer's life. The perverted passion list continues with mention of **impurity**. This reminds us that immorality is "unclean" or dirty and incompatible with the purity of our Savior. Believers are not to be slaves of their **lust** or **evil desires**.[104]

---

[104] Max Anders, vol. 8, Kendell H. Easley, vol. 12, Galatians, Ephesians, Philippians, Colossians, Holman New Testament Commentary, 329 (Nashville, TN: Broadman & Holman Publishers, 1998).

Matthew 5:27-28 Updated American Standard Version (UASV)

27 "You have heard that it was said, 'You shall not commit adultery';[105] 28 but I say to you that everyone who looks at a woman with lust[106] for her has already committed adultery with her in his heart.

Again, this verse is meant for heterosexual relationships; however, what was meant can be useful in controlling same-sex desires, so it will be adapted below.

In verse 28 of Matthew chapter 5, you will notice the phrase "**lustful intent**," keying in on the word "intent." This is not a woman walking along who catches sight of a beautiful woman and has an indecent thought, which she then dismisses. It is not even a woman in the same situation who has an indecent thought, who continues to entertain and cultivate that thought. No, this is a woman that is staring, gazing at a woman with the intent of lusting, and is looking at the woman, **with the intention of** peaking her interest and desire, to get her to lust.

Verse 25 of chapter 26 in Proverbs warns the son against just that, do not get "lustful intent" in your heart because of her beauty. The same is true of a man not getting "lustful intent" in his heart because of the beauty of another man. Yes, even when the evil man is seeking to flame such desires. Aside from the fact that it violates God's Law, you are risking your eternal life for mere moments of immediate gratification at a costly price.

When we view pornography, let alone take up the time to get addicted, we are out for self-gratification, and we are, in no way, reflecting the Christian quality of love. The apostle Paul wrote,

1 Thessalonians 4:3-7 Updated American Standard Version (UASV)

3 For this is the will of God, your sanctification; that is, that you abstain from sexual immorality;[107] 4 that each of you know how to possess his own vessel[108] in sanctification and honor, 5 not in lustful passion, just as also the Gentiles who do not know God; 6 that no man transgress and wrong his brother in the matter because the Lord is an avenger in all these things, just

---

[105] Ex. 20:14; Deut. 5:17

[106] ἐπιθυμία [*Epithumia*] to strongly desire to have what belongs to someone else and/or to engage in an activity which is morally wrong–'to covet, to lust, evil desires, lust, desire.'– Johannes P. Louw and Eugene Albert Nida, *Greek-English Lexicon of the New Testament: Based on Semantic Domains* (New York: United Bible Societies, 1996).

[107] Gr *porneia, fornication*

[108] I.e. body

as we also told you before and solemnly warned you. ⁷ For God has not called us for impurity, but in sanctification.

Pornography especially takes selfish or unfair advantage of women and children and young men, who are likely in abusive situations, for the personal gain of self-gratification. Simply objectifying them for your gratification is demeaning them. If you are using their images, you are also supporting whatever company exploits them, taking advantage of their circumstances. Just taking advantage of images, makes you indifferent, at worst a hater of women and a sexual deviant, toward the very people group that the Mosaic Law and Jesus Christ tried to protect.

Breaking the Habit

Some early Christians, before finding Christ, they were 'unrighteous, sexually immoral, adulterers, men who practice homosexuality, and drunkards.' However, they "were washed, you were sanctified, you were justified in the name of the Lord Jesus Christ and by the Spirit of our God." – 1 Corinthians 6:9-11.

Psalm 55:22 Updated American Standard Version (UASV)

²² Cast your burden on Jehovah,
   and he will sustain you;
he will never permit
   the righteous to be shaken.

This begs the question, how do we throw our burdens on Jehovah (i.e., the Father), and how does he sustain us. How it is that he will not permit the righteous to be moved? In addition, if we are looking at porn, are we not unrighteous? Let us get ever closer to the answer.

1 Corinthians 10:13 Updated American Standard Version (UASV)

¹³ No temptation has overtaken you but such as is common to man; and God is faithful, who will not allow you to be tempted beyond what you are able, but with the temptation will provide the way of escape also, so that you will be able to endure it.

Many Christians, even very mature ones, as well as those leading congregations, have succumbed to pornography. Therefore, you should not feel alone in your battle to get control over your vessel.

Hebrews 4:12 Updated American Standard Version (UASV)

¹² For the word of God is living and active and sharper than any two-edged sword, and piercing as far as the division of soul and spirit, of both joints and marrow, and able to judge the thoughts and intentions of the heart.

This verse contains four statements about God's Word. First, it is **living**. God is a **living** God (Heb. 3:12). His message is dynamic and productive. It causes things to happen. It drives home warnings to the disobedient and promises to the believer. Second, God's Word is **active,** an emphasis virtually identical in meaning with the term **living**. God's Word is not something you passively hear and then ignore. It actively works in our lives, changes us, and sends us into action for God.

Third, God's Word penetrates the **soul and spirit.** To the Hebrew people, the body was a unity. We should not think of dividing the soul from the spirit. God's message is capable of penetrating the impenetrable. It can divide what is indivisible. Fourth, God's message is discerning. **It judges the thoughts and attitudes of the heart.** It passes judgment on our feelings and our thoughts. What we regard as secret and hidden, God brought out for inspection by the discerning power of his Word.[109]

Proverbs 2:1-6 Updated American Standard Version (UASV)

1 My son, if you receive my words
    and treasure up my commandments with you,
2 making your ear attentive to wisdom
    and inclining your heart to discernment;[110]
3 For if you cry for discernment[111]
    and raise your voice for understanding,
4 if you seek it like silver
    and search for it as for hidden treasures,
5 then you will understand the fear of Jehovah
    and find the knowledge of God.
6 For Jehovah gives wisdom;
    from his mouth come knowledge and understanding;

Now, let us return to our questions and provide answers. How do we throw our burdens on God?

We do so by going to him fervently in prayer, asking him for help with the problem we are trying to overcome. Our adding this in our prayers repeatedly shows him our deep concern.

---

109 Thomas A. Lea, vol. 10, *Hebrews & James*, Holman New Testament Commentary, 72 (Nashville: Broadman & Holman Publishers, 1999).

110 The Hebrew word rendered here as "discernment" (*tevunah*) is related to the word *binah*, translated "understanding." Both appear at Proverbs 2:3.

111 See 2.2 ftn.

How Does Ge Sustain Us?

God sustains us by the Word of God, which contains the very knowledge of God, as explained in Hebrews 4:12 above. Thus, we need to discover the Bible verses that are applicable, and we then need to know what the author meant by the words that he used, as should have been understood by his original readers. In other words, we need to discover the original meaning. Then, we need to find the pattern of meaning that would apply to us. This is called working on behalf of our prayers. However, we are not done yet. We must be obedient to the Word of God. If we obey 50 percent, we will get 50 percent results. If we apply it 100 percent into our lives, we will get 100 percent results.

1 John 5:2 Updated American Standard Version (UASV)

² By this we know that we love the children of God, when we love God and do his commandments.

2 John 1:6 Updated American Standard Version (UASV)

⁶ And this is love, that we walk according to his commandments. This is the commandment, just as you have heard from the beginning, that you should walk in it.

> What is love? It plays itself out in the real world in obedience. The essence of love is that we keep God's commandments. This glorifies God, is best for others, and is best for us. Everything God asks of us is intended to give something good to us or keep us from harm. First John presented the same emphasis on love and the same link between love and obedience. (Walls and Anders 1996, 237)

How it is that he will not permit the righteous to be moved?

God said he would never 'permit the righteous to be moved.' What is meant by 'move'?" It means to stumble or fall down spiritually or get into a practice of sin that you seem to be in. In other words, God will help you to become stable, steadfast, or unmovable, not giving into sin. **If we are looking at porn, are we not unrighteous?**

No, this is not the case. We are all sinners, and God hates sin. However, he hates the **unrepentant** practice of sin. The unrighteous person is the one who lives in sin unrepentantly. If you are reading this, and you have been praying, trying to find a way to get control over yourself; then, you are not unrepentant. God makes allowance for our inherited sin from Adam, which means he understands our human weaknesses.

80

Thus, the steps are (1) Go to god fervently in prayer, (2) act in harmony with that prayer, by (3) research what the Bible offers toward recovery, (4) apply what you learn, and (5) get your stride again if you stumble, or get up when you fall down.

How often do you come across pornography?

- Never
- Sometimes,
- Rarely
- Daily,
- Weekly

Where do you come across pornography?

- Television,
- Stores,
- Internet,
- Cell phone,
- Email,
- Work,
- School,
- Other

Do you see a pattern of how these encounters come about, and how you deal with them?

Is there a pattern to your encounters?

Do you find yourself depressed or angry, so you look at pornography because of the feeling that overrides the depression, even though you know, even worse, depression is on the horizon for failing to be faithful? Do you receive email attachments from friends that contain pornography?

The good thing about the internet is that its filters are far better than ten years ago. In order to get a popup or end up with the wrong pages, you need to be very specific in your search. For example, if you Google "race cars," there will be links and images the movement that you get a few letters in. However, if you Google the word "porn," it will do nothing until you hit enter. The same is true with email, like Yahoo and Gmail. The ads in the margins are only reflective of sites that you have been visiting.

How do you react the moment that your eyes see pornography?

- You turn away immediately so that you could barely describe what you saw

- You look at it for a moment before turning away, and could better explain what you saw

- You continue to look until your desires lead you to search for more

The foremost thing that will help you overcome the habit of viewing pornography is to appreciate its seriousness and what your actions mean to you, to God, to your spouse, to your family, and to the victims in the images. You have to get to the point where you "hate evil." – Psalm 97:10.

Remove yourself from whatever results in the viewing of pornography. After one has had success for a time, they become overconfident and think they are strong enough to deal with temptation. This is such a mistaken notion.

Proverbs 22:3 Updated American Standard Version (UASV)

³ The prudent sees danger and hides himself,
but the simple go on and suffer for it.

Be determined that you will not let your eyes fall upon pornography, and if they do unintentionally, you will immediately turn away. When surfing the internet, this is especially important. Each time we encounter someone that stimulates us sexually, it just continues to feed our desires. Each person is tempted when he is lured and enticed by his own desire.

Job 31:1 Updated American Standard Version (UASV)

¹ I have made a solemn promise
never to look with lust at a woman [or man].

Depending on your circumstances, you can apply the following as best you can.

- You only get on the internet when another is in the room

- You will place the computer in a public space

- You will leave your office door open

- You will immediate close out or delete anything inappropriate

- You will find a sponsor that can talk with you when you are feeling weak, stressed, or have stumbled

The Self-Abuse of Masturbation: This subject will be dealt with extensively in a later chapter. The Bible clearly condemns such sexual sins as fornication, adultery, homosexuality, and bestiality; masturbation is not mentioned. (Genesis 39:7-9; Leviticus 18:20, 22-23; 1 Corinthians 6:9-10) Another factor to consider is that the language of the New Testament, Koine Greek, contained several words to describe the practice of masturbation in the Greek-speaking world. Still, they are not used in the New Testament.

While the opinion of most physicians is that masturbation is harmless physically, it seems that the human conscience rejects it, as most are not as comfortable talking about masturbation as they are about another bodily function, like washing your hands. If you doubt me, the next time you are at a restaurant, and the women excuse themselves to freshen up, ask them if they masturbated when they return. If it is natural, you will not have any reservations about asking, and they will not have any embarrassed or angry looks on their face. This may sound extreme, but it makes the point.

Adam and Eve were created in the image of God and were a reflection of his qualities and attributes. Even after the fall, in our state of imperfection, all humans still maintain a good measure of that image. We all have a moral nature, which produces the faculty of conscience. This moral nature and associated conscience are seen in that most countries have laws based on the Bible's moral values, do not kill, do not steal, do not commit adultery, and so on. Why is it that most people feel guilty, ashamed, dirty, embarrassed, or abnormal when discussing masturbation? It is the conscience that God gave us.

Put to Death Evil Desire

Colossians 3:5 Updated American Standard Version (UASV)

⁵ Therefore, Put to death therefore what is earthly in you: sexual immorality, impurity, passion, *evil desire*, and covetousness, which is idolatry.

The ... two words belong together. "Lust" (*epithymia*) and "passions" (*pathos*) or "evil desires," as translated in the NIV, generally refer to strong desires gone bad. Although the word can, on occasion, be used of an honorable desire (1 Tim 3:1), the normal use is negative. It refers most often to the misdirected fulfillment of bodily appetites, usually sexual appetites. A passion is uncontrolled and habitual lust. When lust goes unchecked, a passion for what is forbidden arises. Habits are formed which feed

83

each other. Lust encourages passion, and passion produces more perverted lust.[112]

"Deaden, therefore, your body members," urges the Bible, "as respects . . . **sexual appetite**." (Col. 3:5) This "sexual appetite" is not the new sexual sensation that most youths feel during puberty, of which there is no need to be ashamed. "Sexual appetite" exists when these feelings are intensified so that one loses control. Such sexual appetite has led to gross sexual immorality, as described by Paul in Romans 1:26-27.

However, does not masturbation "put to death" these "evil desires"? Hardly, in order to masturbate, one must feed his mind on evil desires, as well as pornographic images. Like any addiction, it takes stronger content to achieve the same gratification. If you drink one beer a day, soon you will have to move on to two to get the same feeling. If you look at pornographic images, soon they will have to be viler to achieve the same results. Eventually, you will need the real thing because the imagination is not achieving the same outcome. The world is full of opportunity, where you will find yourself aroused in a wrong moment or an inconvenient time, and you will commit fornication if single or adultery if married.

Your Thoughts Will Lead You Astray

Moreover, you're using women or men objectively in your imagination will carry over into the real world. Masturbation means that you need to view and think of women as a tool, as a means to an end, as opposed to sensitive human beings. In addition, you will start to see your own body as an object, a means to self-gratification. Self-abuse is self-centered. The person loses sight of love and moves toward sexual pleasures. Our Creator intended man and woman to find their sexual satisfactions within the marriage bed, between one man and one woman, and within expressions of love.

How does God view our human weaknesses?

Psalm 86:5 Updated American Standard Version (UASV)

[5] For you, O Jehovah, are good, and ready to forgive,
and abundant in lovingkindness to all who call upon you.

---

[112] Richard R. Melick, Jr, vol. 32, Philippians, Colossians, Philemon, The New American Commentary, 291 (Nashville: Broadman & Holman Publishers, 1993).

When we slip up and fall short, succumbing to masturbation, we certainly feel guilty, which is appropriate. However, we do not want to beat ourselves down to where anxiety and stress cause future failures.

1 John 3:20 Updated American Standard Version (UASV)

²⁰ in whatever our heart condemns us; for God is greater than our heart and knows all things.

We may find ourselves falling short on masturbation many times, as it has a stronger hold on us than we may have realized. This results in our feeling guilty, ashamed, dirty, embarrassed, or abnormal. We do not feel worthy of God's Love. We need not think that God is no longer forgiving us, as this is precisely what Satan would like. The fact that you feel as distraught as you do means that God still loves you, and you have not committed the unforgivable sin. Simply be steadfast in the process of overcoming this habit, and continue fervently to go to God in prayer, begging him for forgiveness and cleansing and help. However, we as imperfect humans can be accredited a righteous standing before God, being accepted back into the family of God. **He makes allowances** for our imperfection.

Below is how he views a repentant sinner,

Psalm 103:8-14 Updated American Standard Version (UASV)

⁸ Jehovah is compassionate and gracious,
    slow to anger and abounding in lovingkindness.
⁹ He will not always find fault,
    nor will he keep his anger forever.
¹⁰ He does not deal with us according to our sins,
    nor repaid us according to our iniquities.
¹¹ For as high as the heavens are above the earth,
    So great is his lovingkindness toward those who fear him.
¹² As far as the east is from the west,
    so far does he remove our transgressions from us.
¹³ As a father has compassion on his children,
    so Jehovah has compassion on those who fear him.
¹⁴ For he himself knows our formation;
    he remembers that we are dust.

Isaiah 38:17 Updated American Standard Version (UASV)

¹⁷ Look, it was for my welfare
    that I had great bitterness;
but in love you have delivered my soul
    from the pit of destruction,

for you have cast all my sins
  behind your back.

Micah 7:18-19 Updated American Standard Version (UASV)

18 Who is a God like you, pardoning iniquity
  and passing over transgression
  for the remnant of his inheritance?
He does not retain his anger forever,
  because he delights in lovingkindness.
19 He will again have compassion on us;
  he will tread our iniquities underfoot.
You will cast all our sins
  into the depths of the sea.

You will notice in Psalm 103:12 that God removes the sins of the repentant one as far as the east is from the west. The picture being painted is, to the human mind that is the farthest you can remove something as there is no greater distance. In Isaiah 38, we are given another visual, God throwing our sins behind his back, meaning he can no longer see them, as they are out of sight, thus out of mind. In Micah, our last example, we see that God hurls all of the sins of a repentant person into the depths of the sea. In the setting of the ancient person, this meant that retrieving them was literally impossible. In other words, God has removed them, never to be recovered or brought to mind ever again. This was the viewpoint that he had before Jesus ever even offered himself as a ransom sacrifice.

However, just because God is so forgiving, this will never justify sinning unrepentantly, as his patience will wear out, or the evil age of Satan will end when we least expect it. He hopes that you will continue to work toward setting aside the habit of masturbation, as it is an unclean habit.

Destructive Self-Talk

It is not the troubles of this would that actually cause us to feel bad. It is what we tell ourselves that contribute to how we feel. Self-talk is what we tell ourselves in our thoughts. In fact, it is the words we tell ourselves about people, self, experiences, life in general, God, the future, the past, the present; it is specifically all the words we say to ourselves all the time. Destructive self-talk, even subconsciously, can be very harmful to our mood: mood slumps, our self-worth plummeting, our body feeling sluggish, our will to accomplish even the tiniest of things is not to be realized, and our actions defeat us.

Intense negative thinking will always lead to our feeling blue, painful emotions or even a depressive state. Our thoughts based on a good mood will be entirely different from those based on our being upset. Negative thoughts that flood our minds are the actual contributors to our self-defeating emotions. These very thoughts are what keep us sluggish and contribute to our feeling worthless. Therefore, this thinking is the key to our relief.

Every time we feel down about something, we attempt to locate the corresponding negative thought we had to this feeling down. Because these thoughts have created our feelings of low self-worth, by learning to offset them and replace them with rational thoughts, we can actually change our mood. Remember, the thoughts that move through our mind, with no effort, are the easiest course to follow because we have developed a way of thinking, a pattern of thinking. It is so subconscious that they even go unnoticed because we are not searching for them.

The centerpiece of it all is the mind. Our moods, behaviors, and body responses result from the way we view things. It is a proven fact that we cannot experience any event in any way, shape, or form unless we have processed it with our minds first. No event can depress us; it is your perception of that event that will. If we are only sad over an event, our thoughts will be rational; but if we are depressed or anxious over an event, our thinking will be bent and irrational, distorted and simply wrong.

It may be difficult for us to wrap our minds around the concept that we are responsible for our thinking that leads to most depressive episodes. Still, we are excellent at telling ourselves outright lies and half-truths repeatedly throughout each day. In fact, some of us are so good at it that it has become our reality and led to depression and anxiety. Look at the statements below.

(1) **Self-degrading**: I am gay, or I will never control my desires because I am a pervert. Everything I try seems to fail. Even when I do all I can to control myself, I fail **because I am a failure.**

(2) **Situation degrading**: Life is the same every day; I do not even know why I bother getting up! Life just kicks me in the face every day it stinks!

(3) **Future degrading**: I will never make it in life; I do not know why I even try. It is a waste of time! I will never find happiness like everyone else. Hope, what is that!

We must appreciate that our thinking can deceive all of us, contributing to our belief that the negative mood, which has been created because of our thoughts, is reality when it is not. If we have established a negative way of thinking, an irrational way of thinking, our mind will naturally accept it as truth. We can alter our mood within a moment, and it is not even likely we notice it taking place. These negative feelings feel as though they are the real thing, which only reinforces deceptive thinking.

Talk Therapy for Depression

Talking with a trained therapist is one of the best treatments. Some people choose to be in therapy for several months to work on a few key issues. Other people find it helpful to continue in therapy for years, gradually working through larger problems. The choice is up to you and your therapist. Here are some common types of treatment:

- **Cognitive-behavioral therapy**[113] helps you see how behaviors and how you think about things play a role in your depression. Your therapist will help you change some of these unhealthy patterns.

- **Interpersonal therapy** focuses on your relationships with other people and how they affect you. Your therapist will also help you pinpoint and change unhealthy habits.

- **Problem-solving therapy** focuses on the specific problems you face and helps you find solutions.[114]

---

[113] **Cognitive behavioral therapy (CBT)** is a form of psychotherapy. It was originally designed to treat depression but is now used for a number of mental disorders. It works to solve current problems and change unhelpful thinking and **behavior.**

A Biblical Approach to Cognitive-Behavior Therapy. After pointing out several limitations and criticisms of secular cognitive-behavior therapy, Tan (1987) provided the following guidelines for conducting a Christian, biblical approach to cognitive-behavior therapy that is more broad-based. One guideline is to emphasize the primacy of agape love and the need to develop a warm, genuine, and empathic relationship with the client that is collaborative. Therapists must deal more adequately with the past, especially unresolved developmental issues or childhood experiences, with the judicious use of inner healing prayer or healing of memories where appropriate (see Tan & Ortberg, 1995). They must also pay special attention to the meaning of spiritual, experiential, and mystical aspects of faith and life and not overemphasize the rationalistic dimension. The possibility of demonic involvement in some cases should also be seriously considered. Therapists can use biblical truth and not relativistic, empirically oriented values in conducting cognitive restructuring and behavioral change interventions to modify problem thinking and behaviors. They can also emphasize the Holy Spirit's ministry in producing inner healing and cognitive, behavioral, and emotional change. Prayer and the Scriptures as God's Word will be crucial in this process.

It is useful to pay more attention to larger contextual factors such as familial, societal, religious, and cultural influences and use community and church resources more. Therapists may use only those techniques that are consistent with biblical truth, morality, and ethics and not simplistically use whatever techniques work. They can reaffirm biblical perspectives on suffering, including the possibility of the "blessings of mental anguish" or the "dark night of the soul," with the ultimate goal of therapy being holiness or Christlikeness (Rom. 8:29) and not necessarily temporal happiness. They can utilize rigorous outcome research methodology before making definitive conclusions about the superiority (not just the general effectiveness) of cognitive-behavior therapy, whether Christian or secular. – (Benner and Hill 1985, 1999, 217)

[114] Treatments for Depression - WebMD, http://www.webmd.com/depression/symptoms-depressed-anxiety-12/treating-depressio (accessed April 02, 2016).

We know by now, having come this far in this publication, most of our minor to moderate mental distresses can be overcome by changing the way we think. We also know that the way we think has taken some time to become our thinking pattern and is deeply ingrained by now. However, if we persistently challenge our thinking every time we have an irrational thought, we can unhinge our irrationally, deep-seated ways of thinking.

At first, we will have to be alert to our thoughts because most of them are subconscious and will go unnoticed otherwise. We could carry a small pocket tablet with us to record the times of the day, or how many times in the day we catch ourselves feeding ourselves irrational thoughts and how successful we were in overcoming them. If we fail to take this exercise seriously, it will be like a person with diabetes who refuses his shots, which inevitably leads to significant health issues, even death. The same applies to our mental distress. If we lack trust in the process, it will not be long before we have a major depressive shipwreck and act on our same-sex desires. Below we are going to borrow a powerful section from Matt Moore's blog.[115]

10 Empowering Truths For The Same-Sex Attracted Christian

1) You are not an anomaly. You may have grown up in a culture that taught you homosexuality was the grossest and strangest of sins, but if you're going to believe the Bible, you've got to toss that mentality aside. Your desires are jacked up, yes – but so are everyone else's. Every person's sexuality is perverted by sin. Don't be fooled for a second into thinking you are more sinful than your "straight" friend who is tempted to fornicate, commit adultery, or watch pornography. All are inclined to sin sexually because all have been born with a corrupt nature (Romans 5: 12-21).

2) It's not because you "lack faith" that this struggle remains. There is hellish doctrine floating around in some Christian circles that teaches people their struggle with same-sex attraction exists because their faith doesn't. This teaching is unbiblical and spiritually toxic. You are not still attracted to the same sex because you've yet to believe "big" enough. You suffer this temptation for the same reason all Christians suffer various temptations: because your salvation is not yet complete. You are justified (made right with God), but you are still being sanctified (made like God). Total freedom from sin and temptation will come not on the day that your

---

[115] 10 Empowering Truths For The Same-Sex Attracted Christian, http://www.moorematt.org/10-empowering-truths-for-the-same-sex-attracted-christi (accessed April 25, 2016).

faith finally gets "strong enough" – but on the Day that Christ returns and gives you a new, imperishable body (1 Corinthians 15:53-57).

3) Your identity is not in your fallen desires. You are not defined, even in part, by your fleshly inclinations. Don't identify and view yourself through the lens of your sexuality, but through the lens of your union to Jesus. You're not some different species of Christian. You're not a gay Christian. You are just a Christian (2 Corinthians 5:16-17). You are not the fallen desires you inherited from your first father, Adam. You are the righteousness of God in Christ (2 Corinthians 5:21).

4) You are not alone in your suffering. Sometimes it feels like you're the only Christian that suffers to the degree you do, but this couldn't be more off base. You are not the only one who bears a heavy cross in this life. Your brothers around the world face various, yet equally difficult sufferings. (1 Peter 5:9). Don't give into self-pity; every Christian battles the flesh and has to die to themselves in various ways as they follow Christ (Luke 9:23).

5) God sovereignly rules over your temptations and will not allow them to ultimately defeat you. Your ceaseless wrestling with these desires isn't beyond the grasp of your omnipotent Savior. It may feel at times that the evil inside and around you is going to ultimately overtake you, but Christ who is in you is greater than all the evil, sin, and temptation in and around you (1 John 4:4). Though God allows you to be tempted by these forces, he does not allow you to be tempted beyond your ability to withstand (1 Corinthians 10:13). You *can* resist and you *can* have victory. So fight! And when you don't fight as you should and you stumble (this will happen), don't wallow in the defeat or fear God's judgment. You are justified by the blood of Jesus. All your sins are covered. So get back up and keep fighting. He who called and justified you will not allow your sin to ultimately defeat you. He *will* sustain you to glory (Romans 8:30).

6) God can transform your sexuality. God is not powerless to give you natural sexual desires – even if just for one man or woman whom he's destined to be your spouse. Though heterosexual desire isn't a promise of the gospel, it is not bad to hope for it. And though heterosexual marriage isn't a certainty for anyone, it is not bad to pray God will bless you with it! He has done it for others and he can do it for you. The Lord is a pro at speaking into existence things that don't exist (Romans 4:17). Nothing is impossible for him (Matthew 19:26).

7) Singleness isn't a curse. If God doesn't give you marriage and he calls you be single for the duration of your earthly life, know that he is doing this for your good and joy. God cares for you. If it were better for you to have marriage in this life, he would give it to you. For mysterious reasons that you aren't entitled to know, he may deem singleness the best fit for you. This isn't a curse. It's a freedom and a blessing through which you will serve the Lord more efficiently than you ever could in marriage (1 Corinthians 7:32-38).

8) You can live a full and joyful life without sex. If you're unmarried, your obedience to God in this season of life entails celibacy. Restraining yourself from sexual activity can feel – well, restraining. And it is. You are biologically wired to express yourself sexually, but right now, if you're not married to someone of the opposite gender, it's not an option. Is this hard? Yes. Does this sacrifice rob you of fullness of life? Heck no. Jesus, Paul, and many more like them lived full and joyous lives in the grace of God . . . yet they didn't have sex. It is the pleasures of knowing God – not sex – that truly satisfy the human soul (Psalm 16:11). Eternal life is not found in being romantically or sexually fulfilled, but in knowing and communing with God and his Son Jesus (John 17:3).

9) God will redeem your struggle for his glory. Though the battle with same-sex attraction can be a grueling one, know this: God has a divine purpose for allowing it to continue in your life. Maybe it's to keep you reliant on him. Maybe it's to make your more empathetic toward the struggles and needs of others. Maybe it's to keep you in tune with the brokenness of this world so you keep your eyes on the prize: eternity with Jesus in a new and perfect world. Whatever the case, know for certain that God allows no thorn without a divine purpose (2 Corinthians 12:17). God is using this struggle for your good (Romans 8:28).

10) It won't always be this way. Your struggle will end. The sin inside of you responsible for these attractions will once and for all be obliterated by the redeeming power of God. When Christ comes again, you will no longer just want to be like him but you *will* be like him (1 John 3:2). You will be sinless. You will be perfect. Hold fast to the hope set before you and stand firm in the gospel of your salvation. He who began a good work in you will bring it to completion (Philippians 1:6).

Never Give Up

Many have tried to change their desires, praying, studying the Bible, listening to lectures, putting suggestions into practice, but there has been little success.

There are stories and claims by many thousands who have left the homosexual life and are now living a changed life. Some have made the transition easy enough, while others have had a real fight on your hands. If we want to please God, we must realize that we have to conform to his moral standards, setting aside the former lifestyle, even if it is the most difficult thing we ever face. Do not conform yourselves to the standards of this world, but let God transform you inwardly by a complete change of your mind. Then you will be able to know the will of God, what is good and is pleasing to him and is perfect. Know that God is well aware of the struggle and mental anguish you are going through, and he has compassion for you. (1 John 3:19-20) If we keep God's laws, there is a great reward. (Psalm 19:11) If you prayerfully approach the Bible, the right church leader, and an excellent Christian counselor, you will enjoy the best life possible until Christ returns; after that, paradise.

Therefore, continue to rely on God as you fight those desires. (Gal. 6:9) As Paul said, "Let love be genuine. Abhor what is evil; hold fast to what is good." (Rom. 12:9) In time, even if it seems like a long time, the desires will begin to fade. Just imagine, after the great tribulation, Armageddon, there will be the thousand-year reign of Christ, where your imperfection becomes perfection. After you are 50,000 years into eternal life, will this not seem like a momentary thing of little significance?

CHAPTER 5 Homosexuality – Genes or learned?

Some argue that same-sex attraction is brought about through socialization. Somebody acquires a personality or traits through their background (nurture), impacted by family, friends, school, work, and so on. Others would argue that same-sex attraction is brought about because one is genetically predisposed (nature).[116] They may say, "I am born this way, it is not my fault, why should I be punished, or miss out on love, because of inheriting a genetic predisposition?" We will take on the science of such an issue herein but not as a scientist. Below is a brief article from WebMD News from Health Day by Randy Dotinga

Genetics of Homosexuality in Men

Researchers able to make accurate predictions 70 percent of time in study of twins

THURSDAY, Oct. 8, 2015 (HealthDay News) -- Scientists are reporting that they've linked the way genes in certain regions of the human genome work to influence sexual orientation in males.

The findings don't explain how such variations in the workings of these genetic regions might affect sexuality in one or both genders. But the authors of the new study say they've been able to use this information to successfully predict the sexual orientation of male identical twins 70 percent of the time, compared to the 50 percent that would be expected by chance.

Twins have the same genes, so something else -- such as the way genes operate -- may explain those who don't have the same sexual orientation, the authors suggested.

"Sexual orientation seems to be determined very early in life," said study lead author Tuck Ngun, a postdoctoral researcher at the David Geffen School of Medicine of the University of California, Los Angeles.

---

[116] "A **genetic predisposition** (sometimes also called **genetic** susceptibility) is an increased likelihood of developing a particular disease based on a person's **genetic** makeup. A **genetic predisposition** results from specific **genetic** variations that are often inherited from a parent." – What does it mean to have a genetic predisposition to a .., http://ghr.nlm.nih.gov/handbook/mutationsanddisorders/predisposition (accessed April 16, 2016).

"Based on these findings, we can say that environmental factors might play a role in sexual orientation."

But he doesn't mean the social environment in which we grow up, such as how we're treated by our parents.

"Instead, we are referring to differences that the twins could have experienced in the womb," Ngun explained.

Several past studies have linked sexual orientation to specific genetic regions, "but what's still a mystery is the specific genes that are involved," Ngun said. "Sexual attraction is a fundamental drive across all species but it is something that is poorly understood on the genetic level, particularly in humans."

In the new study, researchers sought to better understand the links between how genes work -- not just the existence of certain genes or genetic variations -- and sexual orientation.

The investigators looked at identical twins because they share the same DNA. However, genes are also affected by the environment each twin experiences, so they're not clones of each other in terms of how their bodies work, according to the researchers.

The researchers began with information on 140,000 genetic regions and narrowed them down to five regions that appear to have the ability to predict -- 70 percent of the time -- whether an identical male twin is gay or straight based on how genes in those regions work or "express" themselves.

The researchers reached that level of accuracy by seeing if they could predict sexual orientation in 10 pairs of male gay twins and 37 male pairs in which one twin is gay and the other is straight, the study said.

"We weren't expecting 100 percent since we are only looking at a small part of the overall picture," Ngun said.

The genetic regions in question play various roles in the body, Ngun explained, including affecting sexual attraction.

Qazi Rahman, a senior lecturer in cognitive neuropsychology at King's College London in the United Kingdom, who studies sexual orientation, praised the study. While it's small, the study's design is strong, he said.

Rahman added that the study "tells us something about possible environmental differences -- albeit biological differences in the environment -- which might explain the sexual orientation of men who share the same genome."

Some people in the LGBT community have expressed concern about research into the biological roots of sexual orientation because they fear it could be used to target gays and even abort fetuses who seem likely to not be heterosexual. "I am gay, so these questions have a lot of resonance with me on a personal level," study lead author Ngun said.

"I do think we have to tread carefully because the potential for abuse is there. Although I think it's highly unlikely that the findings of this particular research study would lead to a genetic test, future research could ultimately lead to something like that," he added.

Society is going to have to work together, Ngun suggested, "to ensure research on sexual orientation is not misused."

The study is scheduled to be presented Thursday at the annual meeting of the American Society of Human Genetics in Baltimore. Research presented at meetings hasn't yet undergone peer review, and is generally considered preliminary until published in a peer-reviewed journal.[117]

This author would argue that science is irrelevant to the Christian faith. Let us err on the side of those who say that, for some, it is genetic, and they are predisposed toward same-sex attraction. If we concede this, it does nothing to remove the Bible's position on same-sex relationships. Remember, the Bible says that we are all mentally bent toward wickedness. We should understand that some lean toward different things in this mental bent and others lean heavily in other directions. By tentatively erring on this side of some being genetically predisposed, we can better help them and better understand their struggles. Lastly, because we accept genetic predisposition, this does not exclude their gaining control over their body and mind and being able to take off the old person and put on the new person. Moreover, it does not exclude that many same-sex attraction cases are socialized.

Further, we could respond that the Bible does not address the genetic predisposition of same-sex attraction, but then again, it does not deal with the mental issues of bipolar either. It is not a science textbook, nor is it a mental health guide. Thus, we should not look for it to resolve the specifics. However, it does address certain thinking and individual actions. Therefore,

---

[117] Scientists Get Closer to Genetics of Homosexuality in Men, http://consumer.healthday.com/health-technology-information-18/genetics-news-334

95

the Bible might not explicitly address the genetic, but it does address same-sex acts.

Another response might be that some have argued that addictive personalities are genetically predisposed (gambling, drugs, alcohol, intense opposite-sex attraction, and pedophilia), as well as anger and rage are also viewed as genetic. Giving these ones the same benefit of the doubt as to the leanings being genetic, would we approve of a man who beats his wife, or another man who sexually abuses women because they may be predisposed to those desires. Certainly not. We would send him to Christian counseling and expect him to get control over his body and mind by putting on the mind of Christ. Would we excuse a genetically predisposed man as a pedophile who acts on his sexual desire for children? No, we would scream, lock him up and throw away the key. We would acknowledge that the wife-beater and the pedophile struggle with these desires, and we would expect that they would **not** put themselves in innocent appearing situations.

Moreover, we would expect them through redemptive therapy through biblical counseling to get and maintain control over themselves. Remember, God feels the same way about homosexuality as the other above sins. We would expect that those with anger issues, those suffering from alcoholism, and those preferring child-sex (pedophile) would get control over themselves and avoid such unsavory activity. God's Word expects the same from those who have same-sex attraction.

Again, the Bible does not directly disclose that same-sex attraction is genetic. However, it could be inferred from God's curse of Canaan (the forefather of the Canaanites), the grandson of Noah, who, it appears, sexually assaulted Noah when he was unconscious from alcohol. It can be inferred that we inherit leanings and dispositions. Certainly, we inherit sin, i.e., imperfection. (Rom. 5:12) In addition, the Bible does say that some of our imperfect traits are deeply ingrained. (2 Cor. 10:4-5) Therefore, if homosexuality is predisposed to some, this does not equate that "God made me this way." It only means it is imperfection passed on like any other. Thus, the fault lies with Satan and Adam. Thomas R. Schreiner deals with this so perfectly and objectively, we will repeat his brief answer again.

Sons and Daughters of Adam

As noted earlier, the biblical prohibition on homosexuality is questioned, because we allegedly have knowledge about homosexuality that was not available to biblical writers. For instance, it is sometimes said that homosexuality is genetic, and biblical writers were not cognizant of this truth. It is not my purpose here to delve into the question of the genetic character of homosexuality. The scientific evidence supporting such a conclusion, however, is not compelling. Most studies yield the rather common sense conclusion that homosexuality is the result of both nature and nurture, and cannot be wholly explained by genetic factors.[118]

However, I do want to look at the perspective of the Scriptures, relative to so-called genetic characteristics. Even if some sins could be traced to our genetics, it would not exempt us from responsibility for such sins. The Scriptures teach that all human beings are born into this world as sons and daughters of Adam, and hence they are by nature children of wrath (Eph. 2:3). They are dead in trespasses in sins (Eph. 2:1, 5), and have no inclination to seek God or to do what is good (Rom. 3:10–11). We come into the world as those who are spiritually dead (Rom. 5:12, 15), so that death reigns over the whole human race (Rom. 5:17). Indeed, human beings are condemned by virtue of Adam's sin (Rom. 5:16, 18). Such a radical view of sin in which we inherit a sinful nature from Adam means that sinful predispositions are part of our personalities from our inception. Hence, even if it were discovered that we are genetically predisposed to certain sinful behaviours like alcoholism or homosexuality, such discoveries would not eliminate our responsibility for our actions, nor would it suggest that such actions are no longer sinful. The Scriptures teach that we are born as sinners in Adam, while at the same time they insist we should not sin and are responsible for the sin we commit. We enter into the world as slaves of sin (Rom. 6:6, 17), but we are still morally blameworthy for capitulating to the sin that serves as our master.[119]

Below is a brief article from Probe Ministries by Sue Bohlin

Is Animal Homosexuality Proof that It's Normal?

First of all, I would encourage her to ask with humility and softness (i.e., no edge in her voice) where she can find the studies that "prove" the prevalence of homosexuality in animals. People toss off assertions all the time (such as, "science has proven homosexuality is genetic") but when we ask where the articles are, they don't have an answer. They're just parroting what they've heard.

---

[118] See, e.g., Stanton L. Jones & Mark A. Yarhouse, *Homosexuality: The Use of Scientific Research in the Church's Moral Debate* (Downers Grove: InterVarsity, 2000); Jeffrey Satinover, *Homosexuality and the Politics of Truth* (Grand Rapids: Baker, 1996); Schmidt. *Straight and Narrow?*, 131–59; Gagnon, *Homosexual Practice*, 396–432.

[119] Thomas R. Schreiner, "A New Testament Perspective on Homosexuality," *Themelios* 31, no. 3 (2006): 70–75.

Same-sex behavior DOES exist in the animal kingdom, for a number of reasons. Usually, it's either playful antics, or dominance behavior to assert hierarchy. For one male to mount, or attempt to mount, another male is a very powerful way to communicate his higher position in the "pecking order" of the community. But if you bring in a female in heat, suddenly the male-male behavior is abandoned in favor of the female. Sometimes males mount other males in a type of practice before the females come into heat.

Secondly, I have read of same-sex attachments in animals, but the fact that they exist doesn't make it normal any more than the fact that cystic fibrosis or diabetes exists makes those diseases normal. From a Christian perspective, we live in a fallen world, and that falleness extends to the entire creation on the planet. It would make sense that things would go wrong even among the animals. For instance, I understand that a hormonal imbalance can result in homosexual behavior in some animals. Here are links to a couple of articles concerning that. Note the naturalistic bias underlying them: "What is, is normal and natural and therefore to be embraced."

http://www.noglstp.org/bulletin/1997spring.html

http://www.libchrist.com/other/homosexual/sheepandanimals.ht ml)

Even from a godless evolutionary perspective, there is no benefit to homosexual behavior since those who engage in it do not reproduce, and from an evolutionary perspective, the only purpose in life is to make babies (the bottom line for the more scientific-sounding "survive and reproduce").

I recently discovered an excellent article on the "animal homosexuality myth" at the NARTH (National Association for the Research and Treatment of Homosexuality) website. This article points out that we can find occurrences of "homosexuality," cannibalism and infanticide in the animal kingdom, but the fact that these aberrant behaviors exist should not lead us to deduce that they are acceptable and normal HUMAN behaviors to engage in!

www.narth.org/docs/animalmyth.html[120]

---

[120] Is Animal Homosexuality Proof that It's Normal?, https://www.probe.org/is-animal-homosexuality-proof-that-its-normal/ (accessed April 25, 2016).

The Origin of Our Troubles

As we have evidenced repeatedly throughout this book, humanity's troubles began with Satan, Adam, and Eve. Indeed, there is no direct responsibility of any of Adam's offspring for Adam's sin. Nevertheless, "just as sin came into the world through one man, and death through sin, and so death spread to all men because all sinned." – Romans 5:12, ESV.

Our imperfection puts us at an apparent weakness. However, that does not mean that we are absolved of our responsibility. Jesus stated, "God so loved the world, that He gave His only begotten Son, that whoever believes in Him shall not perish, but have eternal life." (John 3:16) Paul wrote, "Since by a man came death, by a man also came the resurrection of the dead. For as in Adam all die, so also in Christ all will be made alive." – 1 Corinthians 15:21-22.

Jesus said of himself, "just as the Son of Man did not come to be served, but to serve, and to give His life a ransom for many." (Matt. 20:28, NASB) Paul was extremely grateful for the ransom sacrifice of Jesus Christ. He wrote, "Wretched man that I am! Who will deliver me from this body of death? Thanks be to God through Jesus Christ our Lord! So then, I myself serve the law of God with my mind, but with my flesh, I serve the law of sin." (Rom. 7:24, 25) The apostle John writes, "My little children, I am writing these things to you so that you may not commit a sin.[121] But if anyone does sin, we have an advocate with the Father, Jesus Christ the righteous one" – 1 John 2:1.

Philippians 4:13 Updated American Standard Version (UASV)

[13] I can do all things through him who strengthens me.

> Paul spoke from experience. He had been through the extremes: surplus and poverty. He knew how to weather the dangers of both. This was his secret. Greek and Roman religions had secret initiation rites. Some religions and philosophies prided themselves on secret knowledge. Paul had a different kind of secret. His secret was his reliance on Christ, a reliance gained through his Christian experience. Stoics relied on personal will to gain contentment. Paul did not claim such personal inner

---

[121]   Gr., *hamartete,* a verb in the aorist subjunctive. According to *A Grammar of New Testament Greek,* by James H. Moulton, Vol. I, 1908, p. 109, "the Aorist has a 'punctiliar' action, that is, it regards action as a *point:* it represents the point of entrance . . . or that of completion . . . or it looks at a whole action simply as having occurred, without distinguishing any steps in its progress."

strength. His strength came from Jesus living in him. Paul was in Christ and thus content no matter what his circumstances.

J. Vernon McGee writes:

> Whatever Christ has for you to do, He will supply the power. Whatever gift He gives you, He will give the power to exercise that gift. A gift is a manifestation of the Spirit of God in the life of the believer. As long as you function in Christ, you will have power. He certainly does not mean that he is putting into your hand unlimited power to do anything you want to do. Rather, He will give you the enablement to do all things in the context of His will for you (McGee, *Thru the Bible*, V:327–8).

The Christian life is not only difficult; it is also impossible unless we acquire the power to live it through Christ. To be sure, this truth does not come naturally to us but must be learned.[122]

Life is evidence that we must struggle with major hostile powers, as well as our own sinful tendencies and Satan's efforts to move us off the path of salvation by getting us to stop obeying God. (1 Pet. 5:8) It is also very possible that our genes will affect us in one way or another. Nevertheless, we are certainly not helpless. True Christians have the Father, the Son, and the Holy Spirit, and their gift, the Bible, not to mention the Christian congregation. – 1 Timothy 6:11-12; 1 John 2:1.

---

[122] (Anders, Holman New Testament Commentary: vol. 8, Galatians, Ephesians, Philippians, Colossians 1999, 264)

CHAPTER 6 How do Christians Handle the Transgender Issue?

We start by saying that there are only two genders that God created, male and female. Genesis 1:27 tells us, "male and female he created them." God created only one wife for Adam. (Gen. 2:21-22) The two complimented each other. God commanded man and woman to 'be fruitful and fill the earth' to both Adam and Eve and Noah's family. (Genesis 1:28; 7:7; 9:1; 2 Peter 2:5) Both man and woman were made in the image of God, and they both reflect that image. God depicted himself as a monogamous husband when symbolizing his relationship with the people of Israel. (Isaiah 54:1, 5) This picture is found in both the Old and New Testament

The Word of God stands for all times. God's values, character, and qualities stand the same in infinity. They are not altered because fallen, imperfect man in this fallen world change those values. Homosexuality has existed since Adam and Eve were removed from the Garden of Eden. Over the last few decades, imperfect humans have been working vigorously to revise the genders from two to an unlimited number. The Department has just issued the first U.S. passport with an X gender marker. This will allow a person to choose "X" gender meaning "indeterminate and unspecified" gender. In other words, they do not believe that they are male or female. This has become some transgender theology that has been accepted by some liberal to moderate churches. As has been true of homosexuality, but is also true of transgenderism, it is in direct opposition to the Word of God. For example, Unitarian Universalism is a liberal **religion** with roots in liberal Christianity. It was the first denomination to accept openly **transgender** people as full members with eligibility to become clergy and the first to open an Office of Bisexual, Gay, Lesbian, and Transgender Concerns.[123] This author and truly genuine conservative Christians oppose the ordination of "transgender" and "transsexual" individuals into the clergy. We also oppose the celebration of "transgenderism" as though it was a gift from God. This violates both biology and what the Bible says about there being only two sexes. This distorts being created in the image of God. This distorts that God created them male and female. This distorts that marriage is between one man and one woman. This distorts the family God designed and distorts the society he intended.

---

[123] Office of Bisexual, Gay, Lesbian, and Transgender Concerns Archived 2010-08-13 at the Wayback Machine

Anyone who denies the following biblical claim or goes beyond it, it at odds with God and an enemy of God. He gave humanity two sexes – male and female and stated that marriage is between one man and one woman for sexual love to occur and to procreate and fill the earth.

This new gay and transgender theology directly opposes the Bible and Christian doctrine and the Judeo-Christian values. True Christianity must continue to proclaim the truth of God's Word, not watering it down. Some claim transgenderism and fight for recognition and the rights of male and females, turning the world upside down. For example, "The Center for **Gender Surgery** at Boston **Children's** Hospital offers **gender** affirmation **surgery** services to eligible adolescents and young adults who are ready to take this step in their journey. It is the first center of its kind in the U.S. in a major pediatric hospital setting."[124] So-called transgender children are now offered puberty blockers or hormone treatments once they **reach puberty**. This is child abuse, plain and simple.

Even though the more radical elements of this transgender theology will cancel, verbally and physically assault, and attempt to ruin anyone that gets in their way, most are not of this element. Just as many struggles with same-sex attraction, some struggle with their gender identity. Both groups live in a state of mental and emotional anguish because of confusion, harassment, and rejection. As Christians who are about the business of proclaiming God's Word to make disciples, we do so as Peter and Paul said. We season our words with salt (Col. 4:6), and we do so with gentleness and respect (1 Pet. 3:15) for the people as humans. Of course, we do not water down God's Word, but we also do not beat people over the head with it either.

We are to love our neighbor but not necessarily what our neighbor does. So, we are always willing to talk with anyone about the Bible, carry out a Bible study with them, and invite them to Christian meetings. However, first, we must focus on our own family first. As a young father, I failed in this area, for which I am always deeply pained. I say this because I suffered my own issues as a child, who was sexually abused by four different adults over a decade. This created an inability to cope in society, and I failed my children until they were teenagers. Once I could use the Word of God and cognitive behavioral therapy combined to get my life in order, I have worked very hard ever since in trying to rebuild and build up my children.

Next, we must realize that many who claim to be transgender are confused, and their rejection is not us, so do not personalize the rejection. They reject the Bible because they do not have enough knowledge about it

---

[124] Retrieved Thursday, October 28, 2021 / https://www.childrenshospital.org/centers-and-services/programs/a-_-e/center-for-gender-surgery-program

to make an informed decision. We must also never back down from the fact that there are absolute truths. We must not fear sharing the truths (realities) in the kindest, most respectful way possible, without ever seeming as though we are capitulating to anyone who seeks to "identify" as any gender other than male or female. We must share the actual condition of fallen, imperfect, sinful man. We have said this already. We are all mentally bent toward evil (Gen. 6:5; 8:21), possessing a treacherous heart that we cannot know (Jer. 17:9), whose natural desire is to do wrong. (Romans) This is where their confusion over gender comes from, along with socialization. We must always speak of what the Bible says, as it is our authority, not us. We must state clearly that hormones and surgery cannot change the sex you were born with.

CHAPTER 7 The Pornography Trap

A 50-year-old married physician views Internet pornography for hours at home, masturbating five to seven times a day, then begins surfing porn sites at the office and risks destroying his career.

A woman spends four to six hours a day in Internet chat rooms and having cybersex, and eventually starts arranging to meet online strangers for casual sex in the real world.

A man spends many hours a day downloading porn, filling multiple hard drives, and devotes a separate computer just to pornography.

A married couple views pornographic movies together as part of their loving relationship, but the husband starts spending more time watching and less time with his wife, who feels left behind and rejected.

These scenarios are real-life examples of pornography addiction, a compulsive behavior that falls within the category of sex addiction.[125]

Pornography addiction or problematic pornography use is a behavioral addiction characterized by compulsive, repeated use of pornographic material until it causes serious negative consequences to one's physical, mental, social, and/or financial well-being. Addiction to Internet pornography is a form of cybersex addiction.

Symptoms and Diagnosis

Diagnostic criteria do not exist for pornography addiction or problematic porn viewing. A study on problematic Internet pornography viewing used the criteria of viewing Internet pornography more than three times a week during some weeks, and viewing causing difficulty in general life functioning.

In 1990 Aviel Goodman proposed a general definition of all types of addictions in order to extend the specific disorders included in the DSM-III-R. While not explicitly in the context of pornography, Goodman explains his criteria for addiction as a "process whereby a behavior, that can function both

---

[125] http://www.sfgate.com/health/article/Porn-addiction-destroys-relationships-lives-3272230.php

to produce pain and to provide escape from internal discomfort, [and] is employed in a pattern characterized by (1) failure to control the behavior (powerlessness) and (2) continuation of the behavior despite significant negative consequences (unmanageability)."[126]

According to the San Francisco Chronicle, "If people want to escape feelings of low self-esteem, shame, isolation or the pressures of life, work or relationships, pornography is a place to get lost and feel wanted, imagining the perfect partners who always desires them - and whom they can always satisfy."[127] The Chronicle goes on to say that the risk of job loss and spousal loss is very high for those who are truly addicted to pornography.

Dr. Brown further says, "All too often, sexual addicts risk losing important relationships, being plagued with diseases, and place their jobs and careers on the line. For the addict, it is less about the desire and more about fulfilling a compulsive need."

Prevalence

Though no studies have been conducted on the prevalence of pornography addiction, research on Internet addiction disorder indicates rates may range from 1.5 to 8.2% in Europeans and Americans.[128] Internet pornography users are included in Internet users, and Internet pornography has been shown to be the Internet activity most likely to lead to compulsive disorders.[129] A study found that 17% of people who viewed pornography on the Internet met criteria for problematic sexual compulsivity.[130] A survey found that 20–60% of a sample of college-age males who use pornography found it to be problematic.[131]

---

[126] Goodman, Aviel (1990). "Addiction: Definition and implications". Addiction 85 (11): 1403–8.

[127] http://www.sfgate.com/health/article/Porn-addiction-destroys-relationships-lives-3272230.php#ixzz2N3ZSi4o7

[128] Weinstein, A.; Lejoyeux, M. (2010). "Internet Addiction or Excessive Internet Use". The American Journal of Drug and Alcohol Abuse 36 (5): 277–283.

[129] Meerkerk, G. J.; Eijnden, R. J. J. M. V. D.; Garretsen, H. F. L. (2006). "Predicting Compulsive Internet Use: It's All about Sex!". CyberPsychology & Behavior 9 (1): 95–103.

[130] Cooper, A., Delmonico, D. L., & Burg, R. (2000). Cybersex user, abusers, and compulsives. Sexual Addiction and Compulsivity, 7, 5–29.

[131] Twohig, M. P.; Crosby, J. M.; Cox, J. M. (2009). "Viewing Internet Pornography: For Whom is it Problematic, How, and Why?". Sexual Addiction & Compulsivity 16 (4): 253.

Status as Addiction

In 2011, the American Society of Addiction Medicine published a definition of addiction that for the first time stated that addiction includes pathological pursuit of all kinds of external rewards and not just substance dependence.

The status of pornography addiction as an addictive disorder, rather than simply a compulsivity, is supported by a growing body of evidence but is still contested by some neuroscientists. The current Diagnostic and Statistical Manual of Mental Disorders (DSM-V) includes a new section for behavioral addictions but includes only one disorder: pathological gambling. Other behavioral addictions were included in "Conditions for further study". A 2011 paper by Donald Hilton and Clark Watts argued that studies demonstrating the effect of sexual experiences on neuroplasticity indicate the existence of process addiction, and specifically focused on pornography addiction as an area requiring further study. In a letter to the editor, Rory Reid, Bruce Carpenter, and Timothy Fong responded by arguing that the studies on neuroplasticity used correlational data, and thus could not be used to establish causation. In a commentary included with the letter to the editor, Hilton and Watts pointed to research connecting a marker of addiction, to sexual experience, and claimed that researchers who reject the research they cite are biased against research which connects neuromodulation to behavioral addictions.

Online Pornography

Psychologists who see pornography as addictive may consider online, often Internet pornography, more addictive than ordinary pornography because of its wide availability, explicit nature, and the privacy that online viewing offers. Some claim that addicts regularly spend extended periods of time searching the Internet for new or increasingly hardcore pornography.[132]

Some clinicians and support organizations recommend the voluntary use of Internet content-control software, Internet monitoring, or both, to manage online pornography use.

Sex researcher Alvin Cooper and colleagues suggested several reasons for using filters as a therapeutic measure, including curbing accessibility that facilitates problematic behavior and encouraging clients to develop coping

---

[132] Downs, Martin F.; Louise Chang, MD (reviewer) (August 30, 2005). "Is Pornography Addictive? Psychologists debate whether people can have an addiction to pornography."

and relapse prevention strategies. Cognitive therapist Mary Anne Layden suggested that filters may be useful in maintaining environmental control. Internet behavior researcher David Delmonico noted that, despite their limitations, filters may serve as a "frontline of protection."[133]

Treatment

Cognitive-behavioral therapy has been suggested as a possible effective treatment for pornography addiction based on its success with Internet addicts though no clinical trials have been performed to assess effectiveness among pornography addicts as of 2012. Acceptance and commitment therapy has also been shown to be a potentially effective treatment for problematic Internet pornography viewing.[134]

Breaking the Habit

Some early Christians, before finding Christ, were 'unrighteous, sexually immoral, adulterers, men who practice homosexuality, and drunkards' However, they "were washed, you were sanctified, you were justified in the name of the Lord Jesus Christ and by the Spirit of our God." – 1 Corinthians 6:9-11.

Psalm 55:22 Updated American Standard Version (UASV)

22 Cast your burden on Jehovah,
  and he will sustain you;
he will never permit
  the righteous to be shaken.

This begs the question, how do we throw our burdens on God, and how does he sustain us. How it is that he will not permit the righteous to be moved? In addition, if we are looking at porn, are we not unrighteous? Let us get ever closer to the answer.

1 Corinthians 10:13 Updated American Standard Version (UASV)

13 No temptation has overtaken you but such as is common to man; and God is faithful, who will not allow you to be tempted beyond what you are able, but with the temptation will provide the way of escape also, so that you will be able to endure it.

---

[133] Delmonico, David L. (1997). "Cybersex: High tech sex addiction". Sexual Addiction & Compulsivity 4 (2): 159.

[134] http://en.wikipedia.org/wiki/Pornography_addiction

Many Christians, even very mature ones, as well as those leading congregations, have succumbed to pornography. Therefore, you should not feel alone in your battle to get control over your vessel.

10:13 The final verse of this unit, in contrast to the strong warning of 10:12, offers encouragement for those who seek refuge in the faithfulness of God. From a literary point of view 10:13 is a self-contained, proverbial statement, perhaps inserted as a summary of 10:1–12 and providing a bridge to 10:14. Robertson and Plummer suggest 10:12–13 provides two admonitions; one to the self-confident who think they have no need to be watchful and the other to the despondent, who think it useless to struggle with temptation.[135] Paul does not specify the nature of the temptation, a term that can refer either to an external trial (testing) or to the internal allurement of sin.[136] As a standalone verse the meaning and applications could be wide-ranging, but in context Paul has in mind the allurement of idolatry and associated sins enumerated in 10:6–10, the "craving for evil" that Israel demonstrated in the desert.[137] Such temptations are "common to man," that is, they are not extraordinary trials but the kinds of things experienced by all believers. Garland thinks that what may be in view is external testing in the sense of persecution against those who excluded themselves from the idolatrous feasts.[138]

The phrase "God is faithful" is found also in the letter's opening, where Paul expressed confidence in the Corinthian's final outcome, that God would confirm them blameless in the Day of the Lord.[139] Here Paul relates the phrase to the fact that God will not allow believers to encounter a temptation that they are unable to bear. Not all of the Israelites succumbed to the wilderness temptations, only "some" of them did.[140] The clear implication is that God is faithful to provide the way of escape

---

[135] Robertson and Plummer, *First Corinthians*, 208. So also Thiselton (*First Corinthians*, 749); 10:13 constitutes a warning to the "knowledgeable" in Corinth and comfort to those who are weak in conscience.[135]

[136] Gk. πειρασμός. See Jas 1:2–15 where the term seems to carry both nuances of external trial (1:2–4, 12) and an internal allurement to sin (1:13–15).[136]

[137] So also Thiselton, *First Corinthians*, 747.[137]

[138] Garland, *1 Corinthians*, 467. The verb "to overtake" occurs in other contexts of persecution (see 2 Tim 3:12; 1 Pet 2:19).[138]

[139] For other references to God's faithfulness in Paul, see 2 Cor 1:18; 1 Thess 5:24; 2 Thess 3:3; 2 Tim 2:13.[139]

[140] Cf. Num 14:20–30 and the Lord's commendation of Caleb and Joshua.[140]

for his people in a time of temptation.[141] Sinful though we still are, God's grace is sufficient in every case. The very next verse, 10:14, specifies the way of escape for the situation at hand, "Flee from idolatry!" The path of escape is often a path we are unwilling to take.[142]

Hebrews 4:12 Updated American Standard Version (UASV)

12 For the word of God is living and active and sharper than any two-edged sword, and piercing as far as the division of soul and spirit, of both joints and marrow, and able to judge the thoughts and intentions of the heart.

4:12 For the word of God is living and active.

The word "**therefore**" (*gar*) connects 4:12–13 to the previous statements, as the following section on Jesus as our high priest is linked to these with the word οὖν (*oun*, "therefore;" see 4:14). **The word of God** is given as a powerful aid in entering God's rest. It helps us to become faithful and to remain faithful "holding firmly till the end." Paul wrote,

> Therefore, my dear friends, as you have always obeyed—not only in my presence, but now much more in my absence—continue to work out your salvation with fear and trembling, for it is God who works in you to will and to act according to his good purpose (Phil 2:12–13).

Tobin has demonstrated that the Greek word λόγος (*logos*, "word") "has a wide variety of meanings and is common to all periods of Greek literature, both prose and verse." In general, the NT uses this wide variety. He says:

> It can mean a statement (Luke 20:20), an assertion (Matt 15:12), a command (Luke 4:36), a report or story (Matt 28:15), a proverb or saying (John 4:37), an oracle or prophecy (John 2:22), a speech (Matt 15:12), or the matter under discussion (Mark 9:10; John 14:24).... It can be used of *written* words and speeches, as well as of the separate books of a larger work (Acts 1:1; Heb 5:11).... also ... to mean "ground" (Acts 10:29) or "reason" (Acts 18:14) for something.... In many cases the "word of God" is simply the Christian message, the gospel.

---

[141] Robertson and Plummer (*First Corinthians*, 209) draw attention to the use of the definite article in the phase "the way of escape." It is the necessary way of escape, the one suitable for such difficulty.[141]

[142] Mark Taylor, *1 Corinthians*, ed. E. Ray Clendenen, vol. 28, The New American Commentary (Nashville, TN: B&H Publishing Group, 2014), 237.

Cf. Gal 5:13, "You, my brothers, were called to be free. But do not use your freedom to indulge the sinful nature; rather, serve one another in love."

The "word of God," has been understood in this context to mean (1) Jesus; (2) the Bible; or (3) the message from God. Jesus is called the "the word" in John 1:1 and "the word of God" in Revelation 19:13. "The word of God" is a fitting designation for the collection of sacred Scriptures. But the NT writings were not yet fully collected when Hebrews was written. Furthermore, the *logos* was just mentioned in 4:2 as something that was heard. In 13:7 the readers are urged to "Remember your leaders, who spoke the word of God to you." The message from God has been in the writer's mind from the opening verse (1:1–2, 5, 6, 8, 10, 13; 2:1–2, 6; 3:1, 7, 16, 18). Hence, the third view appears more fitting. The word *logos* appears again in 4:13 in the sense of a settlement of an account. Compare Matthew 18:23 and 25:19.

The Holy Spirit surely works on people's hearts previous to their knowing the gospel (John 16:7–11). Just as surely he who gave us the Bible will work effectively in believing minds that are filled with thoughts from the Bible. One who does not read the Bible is no better off than one who cannot read the Bible. Perhaps he is no better off than one who will not read the Bible. It hardly demonstrates faith in God to ignore the tools he has given us to guide us.

The message of this book is **living and active**. This is no dead, dry, dusty curio. It is **living** (Deut 32:47; Ps 19:7ff.; Isa 55:11) like the living God (3:12; etc.), like the living Son who intercedes for us (7:8, 25). The word stands prominently at the beginning of the sentence. Moulton and Milligan found the word "active" (ἐνεργής, *energēs*) used of a mill that was in "working" order, of "wrought" iron, and of "tilled" land. Lampe found it used in the church fathers to describe an "active" life and a "fervent" prayer.

Sharper than any double-edged sword, it penetrates even to dividing soul and spirit, joints and marrow; it judges the thoughts and attitudes of the heart.

The word of God is "**sharper** than any double-edged sword." Dods says the phrase "sharper than" "is a more forcible comparative than the genitive [by itself]." Then he points to Luke 16:8 and 2 Cor 12:13. The sword was the most widely used weapon of the ancient and medieval worlds. The two-edged sword is a common simile for sharpness (Prov 5:4; Rev 1:16; etc.). Gordon says,

> "The sword … is the most frequently mentioned weapon in the Bible. The earliest swords in the ancient world were usually straight, double-edged and more akin to daggers, being used for stabbing … [In the last half of the 2nd millennium BC]

110

the longer-bladed sword began to be used widely.... In both Testaments the sword is frequently used, by metonymy, for war, or as a symbol for the word of God."

The sword was primarily used for **penetrating** and cutting. Here the focus is on penetration. Beginning with psychological terms, "soul and spirit," the text moves to physiological terms, "joints and marrow." One would expect the reverse order. Finally, the description proceeds to the most secret part of man, "the thoughts and attitudes of the heart." This is so thorough that nothing is hidden from God's sight.

The sword was a feared weapon, often used in threats (Exod 5:3, 21; 15:9; etc.). Perhaps the power of words made the sword an apt image of the tongue. "Reckless words pierce like a sword, but the tongue of the wise brings healing" (Prov 12:18). Jesus is often pictured with a sword coming out of his mouth (Isa 49:2; Rev 1:16; 2:16; 19:15, 21). No one ever spoke with as much power as Jesus.

The phrase, "soul and spirit" is not designed to be a full psychological analysis of man any more than "body, soul and spirit" has that purpose in 1 Thessalonians 5:23. They seem to be simply a way of designating the whole of a person. "Soul" and "spirit" are put in parallel lines as synonyms in Job 7:11 and Isaiah 26:9. The point here is to show that nothing is beyond the penetrating power of the word of God. A sword not only penetrates joints, where bones join, but into the center of the bones, into the **marrow** itself. So powerful is God's word. It penetrates the inmost parts of a person. Those who heard Peter's message about Jesus on the day of Pentecost "were cut to the heart" and cried out "What shall we do?" (Acts 2:37). The jailer at Philippi found the same deep probing of the message (Acts 16:30).

In its irresistible penetration the word **judges** as well. It lays bare the **thoughts and attitudes of the heart.** See Luke 2:35; John 3:19–21; 1 Corinthians 14:22–25. When we read other literature, we are in control. When we read the Bible, it is in control. It lets us see things in ourselves that are otherwise hidden from our own eyes. The Bible pronounces sentence on secret thoughts. We know it knows, and we know it is right in what it discloses. This is exactly what we would expect from literature which God generated. "God knows the thoughts of man" (Ps 94:11). See also Proverbs 15:26. Jesus knew what people were thinking when he was with them even when they did not tell him (Matt 9:4; 12:25; Luke 9:46–48; John 2:23–25). There are no private thoughts and feelings. God knows them all. Dods says,

The word of God coming to men in the offer of good of the highest kind tests their real desires and inmost intentions. When fellowship with God is made possible through His gracious offer, the inmost heart of man is sifted; and it is infallibly discovered and determined whether he truly loves the good and seeks it, or shrinks from accepting it as his eternal heritage.

The **heart** represents the center of one's personal and moral life. "Above all else, guard your heart, for it is the wellspring of life" (Prov 4:23). In the new covenant God writes his laws directly on the heart (8:10; 10:16). At the end of this chapter the author encourages believers to approach God confidently in prayer, but in this approach the heart must be true or genuine (10:22). "Blessed are the pure in heart, for they shall see God" (Matt 5:8). Such hearts are continually being strengthened by God's grace (13:9). The warning not to harden the heart was repeatedly quoted in Hebrews 3–4 (3:8, 15; 4:7). Their hearts were inclined to go astray from God (3:10; Matt 13:15; 15:8; Mark 3:5). The readers, too, are warned against having a sinful, unbelieving heart that turned away from God (3:12).[143]

Proverbs 2:1-8 Updated American Standard Version (UASV)

Wisdom Saves from Evil and Pays Benefits

The Value of Wisdom

2 My son, if you receive my words
  and treasure up my commandments with you,
[2] making your ear attentive to wisdom
  and inclining your heart to discernment;
[3] For if you call out for understanding
  and raise your voice for discernment,

Seek Wisdom as for Hidden Treasures

[4] if you keep seeking her like silver
  and searching for her as for hidden treasures,
[5] then you will understand the fear of Jehovah
  and find the knowledge of God.
[6] For Jehovah gives wisdom;

---

[143] James Girdwood and Peter Verkruyse, *Hebrews*, The College Press NIV Commentary (Joplin, MO: College Press, 1997), Heb 4:12.

from his mouth come knowledge and discernment;[144]
7 he stores up sound wisdom for the upright;
  he is a shield to those who walk in integrity,
8 guarding the paths of justice
  and watching over the way of his holy ones.

1–4. This section also commences with the term *my son*, an indicator of either a family or a school context. The diligence required in the conditions draws attention to the seriousness of the quest for wisdom. Each verse contains a pair of parallel expressions outlining another key ingredient of the search. The first condition (v. 1) is accepting the teacher's words and properly valuing his instructions. The force of receiving or accepting these words is that their teaching must be taken on board or adopted, a deliberate choice not to reject or ignore them, but rather to embrace them (see the parallel in 7:1). The nuance offered in the second half of the verse is that they must be highly valued (ESV, *treasure*; the image is of accumulating something of value) and internalized ('with[in] you'). While the ESV translates the teacher's words as *commandments* (which implies the Ten Commandments and so OT laws), it is better to regard them in a wisdom context as the teacher's commands (so NIV). They are authoritative but not legal commands or instructions.

The conditions continue in verse 2 with an explanation or unpacking of the meaning of accepting and treasuring the teacher's words. It includes paying careful attention to the content of these words, that is, wisdom, and developing a right internal attitude (*inclining your heart*, which refers to the centre of one's being and thinking, not one's emotions).

Verses 3–4 draw attention to the fact that understanding must be actively pursued. There are two different words for understanding in verse 3 (translated by many versions as 'insight' and 'understanding'), both equally common but with no real difference between them. The thrust of the verse is not on describing different subtleties of wisdom, but rather on the verbs. There is a need to pursue understanding energetically, to call out and raise your voice for it. Verse 4 picks up the language of seeking and searching, and again the force rests on the verbs. The quest must be diligently and thoroughly undertaken, based on the belief that what is being sought is of great value. It is to be pursued as if you were desperately searching for lost money, or treasure that is hidden from sight. Indeed, the

---

[144] A Hebrew word frequently rendered "discernment" (תְּבוּנָה tebunah) is related to the word (בִּינָה binah), translated "understanding." Just as is the case with understanding, discernment includes seeing or identifying things, but in the sense of tebunah, it is recognizing and separating the parts, considering, or assessing one in the light of the others.

113

picture that emerges from verses 1–4 is that the quest for wisdom is one that requires great effort and hard work. The willingness to learn in verses 1–2 must be matched by a willingness to work (vv. 3–4). A character shaped by wisdom does not fall into one's lap, but must be actively sought.

5–8. The first consequence of searching wholeheartedly for wisdom is revealed in verse 5, while verses 6–8 outline how God works in his world. The result of striving hard for wisdom is understanding the fear of the Lord and finding the knowledge of God. This was the foundation and starting point in 1:7, but is now also the goal of the process. Knowing God and respecting him as God is clearly not left behind as wisdom is pursued. The search for wisdom will result in knowing and treating God as he is, for this is the ongoing assumption of the godly wisdom promoted by this book. Wisdom is never an end in itself. God's activity is set out in more detail in verses 6–8. He is the giver of what people need to strive for—wisdom, knowledge and understanding. People do not earn wisdom by their own activity, for they are recipients of what God graciously gives. Seeking wisdom involves hard work, but it is not achieved by hard work alone. While OT wisdom literature tends to focus on human actions, the underlying theological presupposition is always that God is working in the background, and usually through human activity to accomplish his active kingly rule. Part of this divine ordering of his world is set out in verses 7–8. He treasures or stores up (*ṣāpan*, the same verb used in v. 1) for the upright the successful use of wisdom skills (esv, *sound wisdom*; niv, 'success'). The second image of verse 7 is that God is a protective shield for those with integrity. There is no explanation at this stage about how God protects or stores up success, but it is clear that this is what he does for those whose character is shaped by uprightness and integrity. It is not a promise of success and protection for the self-indulgent, but for those who respect God as God and who follow the path of wisdom. Verse 8 amplifies the imagery of the shield, stating that God (the continuing subject of vv. 6–8) guards and watches over/protects those who are loyal and who act justly. This means that God is actively involved behind the scenes as people seek to live uprightly.[145]

After reading verses 1-5 of chapter 2, one can clearly see that it is their responsibility to acquire wisdom. *You* or *your* is found eleven times in these first five verses. Each of us is obligated to incline our ear, apply our heart, cry out for, lift our voice, seek, search for wisdom, and then we will understand the fear of Jehovah, the beginning of wisdom, and the knowledge of God we

---

[145] Lindsay Wilson, *Proverbs: An Introduction and Commentary*, ed. David G. Firth, vol. 17, Tyndale Old Testament Commentaries (London: Inter-Varsity Press, 2017), 73–75.

will find. All of this is found in God's Word. What exactly is wisdom though? It is the ability to make sensible decisions and judgments based on knowledge and experience, wisdom is sensibly applied knowledge. The genre of wisdom literature is found all throughout the Bible, but especially in the book of Job, Psalms, Proverbs, Ecclesiastes, and Song of Solomon. However, Wisdom is found in all of the genres of Scripture, even the life lessons within the narrative accounts.

In Chapter 1, Solomon gave his listeners a visual word picture of the consequences for those who do not listen to the corrective words of wisdom, warnings. Here in Chapter 2, he praises the incredible blessings and happiness that wisdom brings. In 2:1-4, Solomon lists three conditional clauses (requirements) that must exist or be brought about before it is possible that one can understand the fear of Jehovah and find the knowledge of God, each beginning with the word "if you (singular)" (vss 1, 3, 4). That is a big "if" because most of mankind pays no attention to God's Word. Clearly, it is up to you to seek wisdom and its handmaidens: discernment and understanding. First, "if you" are going to find joy in studying God's Word, you must be willing to receive Jehovah's words (the Bible) and treat it like it is a treasure that you would never wish to lose, valuing it above all else. **My words** refer to the Law (thoughts and ideas) that Solomon has embraced in an active faith and obedience, which he is teaching as well.

Are you really "attentive" and listening carefully when the Word of God is being explained at your Christian meetings? (Eph. 4:20-21) Do you 'incline your heart [seat or center of the intellect] to discernment' (commit yourself to), which is the insight, good sense, or wisdom to apply God's Word correctly. Of course, in order to incline your heart to discernment, you must be present at Christian meetings. (Proverbs 18:1) Thus, every Christian meeting can be a blessing for you if you are attentive and follow along in your Bibles. (Ac 2:1-4; Heb. 10:24-25. Being attentive means that you are paying attention, taking notice of (maybe taking notes on a tablet), and accepting the information as true, and responding to it.

The second requirement or condition that must exist if we are to understand the fear of Jehovah and find the knowledge of God is to "cry for discernment," which, again is the insight, good sense, or wisdom to apply God's Word correctly. The Hebrew verb here (*qā·rā(')*) has the sense of loud, insistent crying or shouting that one needs help, begging that he be delivered from distress. Wisdom will be ours when our desire gets to the point where we are willing to cry aloud for it. The desperate one 'cries for discernment' to the truth of God's Word and applies it in his life. If we cannot recognize the importance and significance, the fullness of wisdom will elude us. **Discernment** (*bî·nā(h)*) is having the good sense or wisdom to respond

115

properly to the Word of God. **Understanding** (*t<u>e</u>bû·nā(h)*) is having the capacity for discerning a right course of action as the Word of God is applied appropriately. **Discernment** and **understanding** involve comprehending, perceiving, grasping what the authors meant, identifying individual verses in light of the whole, weighing, or evaluating one verse in the light of the others.

The third requirement or condition that must exist if we are to understand the fear of Jehovah and find the knowledge of God is **seeking and searching for hidden treasure**, i.e., be committed and determined in one's quest. History has shown the lengths humans will go to in their quest to discover gold or silver. This makes us think of the mining exploits of men, such as those of the gold rushes in the early United States of American history. Men have spent a lifetime trying to discover gold and silver. What actual value, though, does gold really have? Certainly, we can all agree that the knowledge of God demands far greater dedication, and the treasure of eternal life is a far greater find. The knowledge of God is certainly a spiritual treasure. Therefore, we should have far more zeal as we seek wisdom, discernment, and understanding of God and his will. Solomon likens this knowledge to "hid treasures." The knowledge of God (hidden treasure) will not jump out of its place of hiding and deposit itself into the minds of those who are idle in their quest or search, it requires effort and perseverance on the part of those seeking and searching.

The "her" of **seeking her** and **searching for her** is a reference back to wisdom from verse 2. The imperfect Hebrew verb behind the English **seeking** (*bā·qǎš*) has the sense of diligently acquiring information, trying to get to or reach something that someone greatly desires. This verb is used when one is seeking information from God. (Ex. 33:7) in a similar but figurative sense, one may "seek" the face of God. (2 Sam. 21:1) Here (*bā·qǎš*) is used in reference to our searching for information, that is, a mental pursuit. The imperfect Hebrew verb behind the English **searching** (*hā·p̄ǎš*) has the sense of searching for, examining, trying to locate or discover information, in this case about the wisdom of God. The Hebrew noun behind the English **treasures** (*mǎṭ·môn*) has the sense of something of value that is hidden.

Searching for treasures requires discipline and determination. It calls for much digging be it actual treasure or seeking and searching for the knowledge of God, for "discernment," and for "understanding." This also demands much digging or getting below the surface knowledge. It is not sufficient to skim over the surface of God's Word. The invaluable treasures of the knowledge of God are for all who, like a determined, tenacious, resolute treasure hunter, are willing to seek them. Are we persistent in finding the knowledge of God? How can we improve our ability in doing so? Certainly, accurate knowledge of God and his Word is like a hidden treasure. What

116

could be more valuable than the knowledge of God and Christ, which leads to eternal life? (John 17:3) Again, this treasure must also be sought for and discovered. Then, it must also be retained. It can also be expanded or grown. All of this means much effort on our part.

If you fulfill these three "if you" requirements or conditions of verses 1, 3, 4 and keep searching for, examining, trying to locate or discover information for wisdom, God says that you will finally understand the fear of Jehovah but will also find the knowledge of God. You are promised that you will gain God (2:5-8), and you will attain the wisdom of God. (2:9-11) The person searching for wisdom will find far more than mere human wisdom, as God is the source of all wisdom. When you enter the path that takes you deeper and deeper into the wisdom of God, you will find the very knowledge of God at the end of the path. When we recognize and accept the sovereignty of God, the fear of Jehovah, you will be ready to truly listen and accept him. Solomon identifies this treasure for you as "the knowledge of God," specifically, the truth about God and his will and purposes as revealed in the Bible. (2:5) There are numerous aspects to this treasure: true teachings, wise counsel, insight into the nature of God and his personality, as well as what lies ahead, and much more.

Jehovah represents himself symbolically as having a **mouth** (Heb. *pě(h)*) to convey to the reader about his communication, speech that gives you information, exhortation, counsel, or commands, which are contained in Scripture, wherein God speaks to you. (cf. Heb. 1:1-2; 2 Pet. 1:20-21) The **upright** (Heb. *yā·šār*) are God's true believers, his holy ones, who are diligently seeking and searching to know, love, and obey God and to live righteously as one can within their human imperfection. (Gen. 6:5; 8:21; Jer. 17:9; Rom. 5:12) You, the **holy one** is keeping the new covenant (Jer. 31.31; Heb. 8:8-12); thus, you know **wisdom**, which has served as a **shield** (Heb. *mā·ḡēn*) of defense from the offensive weapons of Satan, the world, and your own human imperfection, as you **walk** (Heb. *hā·lăḵ*) in **integrity** (Heb. *tōm*) a state of blamelessness being free of guilt, **guarding** (Heb. *nā·ṣǎr*) you, making you safe from danger within your relationship with Jehovah (Ps 40:12) on the **paths of justice, watching** (Heb. *šā·mǎr*) over them. Hebrew terms relating to integrity have the root meaning of that which is "whole" or "complete." They often suggest moral soundness and uprightness. Those walking in **integrity** are unbending in devotion to Jehovah. For such blameless ones, he is a protective shield because they display true wisdom and conform to his righteous standards. This does not mean, though, that Jehovah will not allow you to be tested. He did so even with Job. "God is faithful," the apostle Paul noted to the Corinthians. In full he said, "No temptation has overtaken you but such as is common to man; and God is faithful, who will not allow you to be tempted beyond what you are able, but with the temptation will provide the way of escape also, so that you will be able to endure it." – 1 Corinthians 10:13.

Jehovah God will give wisdom to those, who are seeking and searching as though it were a hidden treasure. Imagine a gold mine on the side of a hill. If someone wanted enough money to have a meal or two, without working too hard, he could just pick up some specs of gold on the hillside. However, if he wanted a lifetime of meals, a life of financial security, he would be working in the mine daylight to dark. Sadly, when those searching for treasure crossed America to California in 1849, in search of gold, they soon discovered that the odds of striking it rich were ten thousand to one. It is quite different from Jehovah God, as he gives wisdom to all, "from his mouth come knowledge and understanding." Yes, God gives out wisdom free; he is the mine, for those that want to be wise.

We need to make this a part of our prayer life. The psalmist prayed, "Teach me your way, O Jehovah, that I may walk in your truth; unite my heart to fear your name." (Psalm 86:11) This is one prayer that we know will be answered. However, the answer will be based on the level that we act in harmony with our prayers. Are we willing to buy out the time to acquire wisdom, understanding, and discernment? A mere 30-60 minutes a day of Bible study will bring results that one might not have ever imagined. Are we willing to work 30 years to pay off a house, 40-45 years to receive a social security check (USA), but not 30-60 minutes a day, to acquire the wisdom of God that leads to eternal life?

CHAPTER 8 The Self-Abuse of Masturbation

Masturbation is the sexual stimulation of one's own genitals, usually to the point of orgasm.

Is masturbation serious? Some Bible scholars view masturbation, saying, "The Hebrew and Christian Bibles are silent, neither denouncing nor encouraging the practice. The biblical story of Onan is traditionally linked to referring to masturbation and condemnation thereof, but the act described by this story is coitus interruptus, not masturbation."[146] Protestant "Theologians toward the middle of the 20th century began revising previous teachings, and some today even take pro-masturbation viewpoints. Some view it as an act of self-indulgence and even a sin of the flesh and believe that the practice is principally considered a sin because of its invitation to lust.[147] Those who view it within the range of allowable sexual behavior encourage it as a guard against adultery, pre-marital sex, or other forms of non-allowable sexual behavior, and as a method of balancing differing libidos between spouses."[148]

Before delving into the problems of masturbation, we should consider some things first. God gave men and women the natural desires of sexual attraction and physical pleasures, which are a result of stimulating certain parts of the body. However, Adam and Eve naturally leaned toward good and would have perfect control over their sexual desires. In fact, they did not even have clothes and went around naked. The first couple was together for a long time in the Garden of Eden before they sinned and were expelled. It would seem that they never had relations throughout that time, as they would have likely procreated and had children in the Garden of Eden.[149] Their desire for sexual attraction would not have been as dysfunctional as imperfect humans after the fall when sin entered the world. They were busy carrying out the duties that God had given them, like naming the animals, caring for

---

[146] Coogan, Michael (October 2010). God and Sex. What the Bible Really Says (1st ed.). New York, Boston: Twelve. Hachette Book Group. p. 110.

Ellens, J. Harold (2006). "6. Making Babies: Purposes of Sex". Sex in the Bible: a new consideration. Westport, Conn.: Praeger Publishers. p. 48.

[147] Miller, Jeff (2008). "Masturbation". Bible.org.

[148] Wright, Anne (2009). Grandma's Sex Handbook. Intimate Press. pp. 123–146.

[149] For a discussion on the length of the creation days, please see, http://bible-translation.net/page/part-2-genesis-1-1-is-the-earth-only-6-000-to-10-000-years-old-are-the-creative-days-literally-only-24-hours-long

the garden, knowing there was an eternity for the procreation, but knowing that they would sin one day. – Romans 5:12.

Because Adam and Eve rebelled against the sovereignty of God, sin entered into the world. This means sexual desires were just the opposite of their descendants, for we have inherited the disease of sin, missing the mark of perfection. (Gen. 6:5, AT) "When the Lord saw that the wickedness of man on the earth was great and that **the whole bent of his thinking was never anything but evil . . . ."** (Gen. 8:21, AT) ". . . **the bent of man's mind may be evil from his very youth. . . ."** (Jer. 17:9, ESV) The **heart is deceitful** above all things, and it is exceedingly corrupt: who can know it?

The main reason for sexual intercourse between a man and a woman is to procreate and fill the earth. Being that God is the Creator of all, including humans, he has the right to set the moral standards of what is good and what is bad. Of Course, Adam and Eve disregarded this when their rebellion demonstrated that they felt that they did not need his standards but could determine for themselves what is good and what is bad. The Bible is quite clear that sexual relations are to be between one man and one woman, who are married. Anything outside of that would be adultery if married or fornication if unmarried.

The imperfect human lacks the self-control that perfect Adam and Eve displayed. Those who are single have sexual desires that are not able to be satisfied. In fact, the male human body has a way of dealing with such stress to the body, which is by nocturnal emission of semen. Is masturbation another way for single men and women to deal with the stress and frustration of pent up sexual desires? No. While it is true that masturbation does no physical harm if practiced in moderation. However, as Christians, we are not concerned with the physical aspect but rather the spiritual aspect.

The Bible on Masturbation

The Bible clearly condemns such sexual sins as fornication, adultery, homosexuality, and bestiality; masturbation is not mentioned. (Genesis 39:7-9; Leviticus 18:20, 22-23; 1 Corinthians 6:9-10) Another factor to consider is that the language of the New Testament, Koine Greek, contained several words to describe the practice of masturbation in the Greek-speaking world. Still, they are not used in the New Testament.

Adam and Eve were created in the image of God and were a reflection of his qualities and attributes. Even after the fall, in our state of imperfection, all humans still maintain a good measure of that image. We all have a moral nature, which produces the faculty of conscience. This moral nature and associated conscience are seen in that most countries have laws based on the Bible's moral values, do not kill, do not steal, do not commit adultery, and so on. Why is it that most people feel guilty, ashamed, dirty, embarrassed, or abnormal when discussing masturbation? It is the conscience that God gave us.

Put to Death Evil Desire

Colossians 3:5 Updated American Standard Version (UASV)

⁵Therefore, Put to death therefore what is earthly in you: sexual immorality, impurity, passion, *evil desire*, and covetousness, which is idolatry.

> The … two words belong together. "Lust" (*epithymia*) and "passions" (*pathos*) or "evil desires," as translated in the NIV, generally refer to strong desires gone bad. Although the word can, on occasion, be used of an honorable desire (1 Tim 3:1), the normal use is negative. It refers most often to the misdirected fulfillment of bodily appetites, usually sexual appetites. A passion is uncontrolled and habitual lust. When lust goes unchecked, a passion for what is forbidden arises. Habits are formed which feed each other. Lust encourages passion, and passion produces more perverted lust.[150]

"Deaden, therefore, your body members," urges the Bible, "as respects ... **sexual appetite**." (Col. 3:5) This "sexual appetite" is not the new sexual sensation that most youths feel during puberty, of which there is no need to be ashamed. "Sexual appetite" exists when these feelings are intensified so that one loses control. Such sexual appetite has led to gross sexual immorality, as described by Paul at Romans 1:26-27.

However, does not masturbation "put to death" these "evil desires"? Hardly, in order to masturbate, one must feed his mind on evil desires, as well as pornographic images. Like any addiction, it takes stronger content to achieve the same gratification. If you drink one beer a day, soon you will have to move on to two to get the same feeling. If you look at pornographic images, soon they will have to be viler to achieve the same results. Eventually, you will need the real thing because the imagination is not achieving the same outcome. The world is full of opportunity, where you will find yourself aroused in a wrong moment or an inconvenient time, and you will commit fornication if single or adultery if married.

---

[150] Richard R. Melick, Jr, vol. 32, Philippians, Colossians, Philemon, The New American Commentary, 291 (Nashville: Broadman & Holman Publishers, 1993).

Your Thoughts Will Lead You Astray

Moreover, your using women or men objectively in your imagination will carry over into the real world. Masturbation means that you need to view and think of women as a tool, as a means to an end, as opposed to sensitive human beings. In addition, you will start to see your own body as an object as well, a means to self-gratification. Self-abuse is self-centered. The person loses sight of love and moves toward sexual pleasures. Our Creator intended man and woman to find their sexual satisfactions within the marriage bed, between one man and one woman, and within expressions of love.

How Does God View our Human Weaknesses?

Psalm 86:5 Updated American Standard Version (UASV)

⁵ For you, O Jehovah, are good, and ready to forgive,
and abundant in lovingkindness to all who call upon you.

When we slip up and fall short, succumbing to masturbation, we certainly feel guilty, which is appropriate. However, we do not want to beat ourselves down to where anxiety and stress cause future failures.

1 John 3:20 Updated American Standard Version (UASV)

²⁰ in whatever our heart condemns us; for God is greater than our heart and knows all things.

We may find ourselves falling short on masturbation many times, as it has a stronger hold on us than we may have realized. This results in our feeling guilty, ashamed, dirty, embarrassed, or abnormal. We do not feel worthy of God's Love. We need not think that God is no longer forgiving us, as this is exactly what Satan would like. The fact that you feel as distraught as you do means that God still loves you, and you have not committed the unforgivable sin. Simply be steadfast in the process of overcoming this habit, and continue fervently to go to God in prayer, begging him for forgiveness and cleansing and help. However, we as imperfect humans can be accredited a righteous standing before God, being accepted back into the family of God. **He makes allowances** for our imperfection.

Below is how he views a repentant sinner,

Psalm 103:8-14 Updated American Standard Version (UASV)

⁸ Jehovah is compassionate and gracious,
    slow to anger and abounding in lovingkindness.
⁹ He will not always find fault,

nor will he keep his anger forever.

¹⁰ He does not deal with us according to our sins,
  nor repaid us according to our iniquities.
¹¹ For as high as the heavens are above the earth,
  So great is his lovingkindness toward those who fear him.
¹² As far as the east is from the west,
  so far does he remove our transgressions from us.
¹³ As a father has compassion on his children,
  so Jehovah has compassion on those who fear him.
¹⁴ For he himself knows our formation;
  he remembers that we are dust.

Isaiah 38:17 Updated American Standard Version (UASV)

¹⁷ Look, it was for my welfare
  that I had great bitterness;
but in love you have delivered my soul
  from the pit of destruction,
for you have cast all my sins
  behind your back.

Micah 7:18-19 Updated American Standard Version (UASV)

¹⁸ Who is a God like you, pardoning iniquity
  and passing over transgression
  for the remnant of his inheritance?
He does not retain his anger forever,
  because he delights in lovingkindness.
¹⁹ He will again have compassion on us;
  he will tread our iniquities underfoot.
You will cast all our sins
  into the depths of the sea.

You will notice in Psalm 103:12 that God removes the sins of the repentant one as far as the east is from the west. The picture being painted is, to the human mind that is the farthest you can remove something as there is no greater distance. In Isaiah 38, we are given another visual, God throwing our sins behind his back, meaning he can no longer see them, as they are out of sight, thus out of mind. In Micah, our last example, we see that God hurls all of the sins of a repentant person into the depths of the sea. In the setting of the ancient person, this meant that retrieving them was literally impossible. In other words, God has removed them, never to be retrieved or brought to mind ever again. This was the viewpoint that he had before Jesus ever even offered himself as a ransom sacrifice.

However, just because God is so forgiving, this will never justify sinning unrepentantly, as his patience will wear out, or the evil age of Satan will end when we least expect it. He hopes that you will continue to work toward setting aside the habit of masturbation, as it is an unclean habit.

CHAPTER 9 Can the Bible Help Us Cope with Loneliness?

Intense feelings of loneliness can be so overwhelming it could lead to alcoholism, drug abuse, even suicide. If it drags on for weeks, it would be best to seek the help of a Christian counselor. The world seems so crowded in the 21st century, especially because of the internet. One might ask, how could anyone feel alone? First, it should be noted upfront that some feelings of loneliness are appropriate at certain times. For example, the husband is away on a business trip, or a child heads off to college, or the elderly husband or wife is left at home while the other has to go to a nursing home.

Some believe that "if I just surround myself with friends and family members, I will get over this bout of loneliness.' While this may provide a measure of distraction, it does not always solve the problem because there is a void. We cannot spend time with friends every minute of every day. Some have even made the error of believing that marriage would be the answer, so they rush into a marriage, which ends up as a life of loneliness, as a married person. One has to conquer the missing component of their loneliness before they can enjoy the relationship with another.

The Correct Mindset

The Bible offers its readers, who correctly apply its counsel, practical advice on coping with loneliness. While we have all felt the pain of loneliness, some more so than others, being alone is not necessarily equal to loneliness. Even Jesus wanted some alone time, Matthew 14:13 tells us that Jesus 'withdrew to a secluded place to be by himself.' He wanted the alone time to rest from the crowds, to meditate, and pray.

Mark 6:31 Updated American Standard Version (UASV)

31 31 And he said to them, "Come away by yourselves to a isolated place and rest a while." For many were coming and going, and they did not even have time to eat.[151]

---

[151] With this verse, Mark resumes his narrative about the disciples whom Jesus had sent out. The disciples returned and they had an exciting tale to tell. But the crowds were increasing by such large numbers (partly due to the disciples' actions) that they had not even had a chance to eat. The large crowds suggest that Jesus and his disciples were probably in Capernaum.

Jesus knew how tiring ministry can be. He knew what it felt like to heal people, to have the press of the crowds upon him, to preach from town to town until his voice was hoarse, to get so caught up in God's business that daily needs were forgotten. His compassion reached out to the disciples, and he encouraged them to come away from the crowds to get some rest. – (Cooper 2000, 105)

If our circumstances have us living alone, we do not view it from a lonely perspective. What we tell ourselves in our self-talk about our being alone will develop into how we feel. We need to view our alone time as a blessing from God and take a few moments, reflecting on how we use our alone time. Are we simply looking for ways to fill the time before our next encounter with people? Alternatively, we could contemplate how we might better use this alone time to make the most out of it.

We can use our alone time to take care of our responsibilities around the house. If we work hard all day, we can use some of our alone time to recharge physically, emotionally, and spiritually by taking a long hot bath and planning a movie and a snack that is mentally encouraging and healthy. We can use some of our alone time for personal Bible study to prepare for Christian meetings. The apostle Paul tells us, "the word of God is living and active, sharper than any two-edged sword, piercing to the division of soul and of spirit, of joints and of marrow, and discerning the thoughts and intentions of the heart." – Hebrews 4:12.

True Friends

Proverbs 18:24 Updated American Standard Version (UASV)

24 A man of many friends will be broken in pieces,
but there is a friend who sticks closer than a brother.

While alone time is great for getting things done, digging into the Word of God, and rebooting for the next day, we were designed for companionship. In other words, humans were designed to be people persons. While being with a group, having a good time can be refreshing, it need not always be a group to set aside feelings of loneliness. It can simply be a few close friends who help you see that you are truly not alone.

There are some, who struggle to make friends. We may want to do a little self-examination about why we struggle to acquire friends and maintain that friend after that. Some want an enormous amount out of friendship while they do not reciprocate hardly anything in return. These ones suck the very life out of a friendship because they are excessively needy. They tend to isolate themselves until they cannot stand it any longer, and then call on a friend, to which they go on and on in a rapid-fire conversation about one problem after another.

Proverbs 18:1 Updated American Standard Version (UASV)

18 Whoever isolates himself seeks his own desire;
he breaks forth against all sound wisdom.

If we are suffering from loneliness, we may want to start with self-examination. What am I doing with my downtime? How can I use it more wisely? How can I look at it in a different light? Who are my real friends, and am I giving them as much as I am getting? Do I demonstrate that I am as interested in them as they are in me? Alternatively, Do I tend to focus all of the attention on myself? If we are to disrupt the phase of loneliness, we will have to become more of a giver and less of a receiver.

Philippians 2:4 Updated American Standard Version (UASV)

⁴ Everyone should look out not only for his own interests,¹⁵² but also for the interests of others.

> Looking out for our own interests comes naturally. We need, and receive, no instruction for that. We are instructed to look out for **the interests of others**. We are to keep an eye out to discover ways we can help others even when they do not see they need such help. The apostle stated in Galatians 6:2: "Carry each other's burdens, and in this way you will fulfill the law of Christ."¹⁵³

If we were to "look out for" the interests of others, this would include an emotional and spiritual reflection of or plot for the best time to demonstrate our interest in them. Thus, we can consider our family, our friends, and congregation members, reflecting on their needs, plotting how we might fill those needs. If all of us look out for the needs of others, be it mental, emotional, physical, or spiritual needs; then, others will meet our needs.

If we are to have a close, intimate friend, we must first be a close, intimate friend. Jesus said, "Give, and it will be given to you … For with the measure you use it will be measured back to you." (Luke 6:38) In addition, the apostle Paul says Jesus said, "'it is more blessed to give than to receive.'"--Acts 20:35

We are Never Ever Truly Alone

Matthew 5:3 Updated American Standard Version (UASV)

³ "Blessed¹⁵⁴ are the poor¹⁵⁵ in spirit, for theirs is the kingdom of the heavens.

---

¹⁵² Lit not the (things) of themselves each (ones).

¹⁵³ http://biblia.com/books/hntc69ga/Php2.4

¹⁵⁴ I.e. fortunate or prosperous

¹⁵⁵ "Blessed are those who [are poor in spirit] recognize they are spiritually helpless …" (GOD'S WORD Translation) The Greek word *ptochos* means "beggar." The "poor in spirit" is an alternative literal

127

In any century, a poor person has little reason to be happy, based on outward circumstances. Jesus, however, clarified in the first words of his sermon that he was not speaking of physical poverty, but spiritual poverty—**poor in spirit**. The beginning of repentance is the recognition of one's spiritual bankruptcy—one's inability to become righteous on one's own. The blessing or happiness that belongs to the poor in spirit is because such a person is, by his admission, already moving toward participating in God's kingdom plan, acknowledging his need for a source of salvation outside himself. Old Testament uses of this concept would have been familiar to Jesus' listeners and Matthew's readers. (Familiar Scriptures would have included Pss. 40:17; 69:29–30, 33–34; Isa. 57:15; 61:1; 66:2, 5.)[156]

Yes, we need to be aware of our spiritual needs. We were created with the need to develop a friendship with our Creator. One thing is for certain, humans may fail us, but God never will. Therefore, we can feel secure in that friendship, like no other. Jesus said,

John 16:32 Updated American Standard Version (UASV)

[32] Behold, the hour is coming, indeed it has come, when you will be scattered, each to his own home, and will leave me alone; and yet **I am not alone, for the Father is with me**.

Our friendship with God can quench our loneliness. However, this will not be the case, if we treat God like was stated above, expecting him to be the only giver in the friendship. We must develop the friendship with God, by getting to know him, to draw closer to him.

Psalm 34:8 Updated American Standard Version (UASV) [8] Oh, taste and see that Jehovah is good! Happy[157] is the man who takes refuge in him!	**John 17:3** Updated American Standard Version (UASV) [3] This is eternal life, that they may know you, the only true God, and the one whom you sent, Jesus Christ

rendering. The meaning is that the "beggar/poor in spirit" is aware of his or her spiritual needs, as if a beggar or the poor would be aware of their physical needs.

[156] http://biblia.com/books/hntc61mt/Mt5.3

[157] **Happy, blessed is**: (Heb. *asre*; Gr. *makarios*) *Asre* occurs 11 times in the Hebrew Old Testament and *makarios* 50 times in the Greek New Testament. Happiness and being highly favored by God characterize this joy. It is speaking of a person who is content, full of joy. This is not to be confused with the Hebrew word *barak* which means, "to bless," as in a divine blessing. The Hebrew barak and the Greek *eulogeo* is the act of being blessed, while the Hebrew *asre* and Greek *makarios* is the state or condition of the person who is being blessed, who is a highly favored one. – 1 Ki 10:8; Ps 1:1; 119:1-2; Pro. 14;21; 16:20; Matt. 5:3-11; 11:6; 13:16; Lu 1:45; John 13:17; 20:29; Ac 20:35; Rom. 4:7-8 to mention just a few.

While the above counsel can get one out of the pits of loneliness, it is paramount that we seek help if we are falling deeper and deeper into depression, especially if we have had thoughts of hurting ourselves.[158]

---

[158] www.aacc.net/

CHAPTER 10 Why has God Permitted Wickedness and Suffering?

"God has morally sufficient reasons for permitting the evil and suffering in the world." – William Lane Craig

That *morally sufficient reason* lies below.

"The significant issue that drove me to Agnosticism [Bible Scholar Dr. Bart D. Ehrman is now an Agnostic] has to do not with the Bible, but with the pain and suffering in the world." He writes, "I eventually found it impossible to explain the evil so rampant among us—whether in terms of genocides (which continue), unspeakable human cruelty, war, disease, hurricanes, tsunamis, mudslides, the starvation of millions of innocent children, you name it—if there was a good and loving God who was actively involved in this world." *Misquoting Jesus* (p. 248)

As you will see below, Ehrman's issue is simply a matter of starting with the wrong assumption. **Point One**: He starts with 'if God is a God of love, who has the power to fix anything, how can there have been such horrific pain and suffering in imperfection over the last 6,000 years?' **Point Two**: He also likely begins with the premise that 'God is responsible for everything that happens.' If one starts with the wrong assumption, there is no doubt that he will reach the wrong conclusion(s). **Point One** is dealt with below, but let it be said that Ehrman is looking through the binoculars from the opposite end, the big side through the small. When we do that, we get a narrow, focused outlook. God looks through the binoculars the correct way and can see the big picture. Ehrman can only see but a fraction and a moment of time, 70 – 80 years, while God has seen everything that has happened over these past 6,000 plus years in the greatest of detail, and can see what the outcome would be if he had handled things in a variety of ways.

Point Two is certainly one reason suffering and evil is often misunderstood. God is responsible for everything, but not always directly. If he started the human race and ended up with what we now have, he is essentially **indirectly** responsible. Parents who have a child are similarly accountable for the child committing murder 21 years into his life because they procreated and gave birth to the child. The mother and father are **indirectly** responsible. King David commits adultery with Bathsheba, has her husband Uriah killed to cover things up, and impregnates Bathsheba, but the adulterine child, who remains nameless, dies. Is God responsible for the death of that child? We can answer yes and no to that question. He is responsible in two ways: **(1)** He created humankind, so there would have been no affair, murder, adulterine child if he had not. **(2)** He did not step in and save the child when he had the power to do so. However, he is not directly responsible because he did not make King David and Bathsheba commit the acts that led to the child being born, nor did he bring an illness on the adulterine child. He just did not move in to protect the child in a time that had a high rate of infant deaths.

The reason people think that God does not care about us is the words of some religious leaders, which have made them feel this way. When tragedy strikes, what do some pastors and Bible scholars often say? When 9/11 took place, with thousands dying in the twin towers of New York, many ministers said: "It was God's will. God must have had some good reason for doing this." When religious leaders make such comments or similar ones, they are actually blaming God for the bad things that happened. Yet, the disciple James wrote, "Let no one say when he is tempted, 'I am being tempted by God,' for God cannot be tempted with evil, and he himself tempts no one." (James 1:13) God never directly causes what is bad. Indeed, "far be it from God that he should do wickedness, and from the Almighty that he should do wrong." Job 34:10.

The history of humans has been inundated with pain and suffering on an unprecedented scale, much of which they have brought on themselves. The problem/question that has plagued many persons is, 'why if there is a loving God, would he allow it to start with, and worse still, why allow it to go on for over 6,000 years?' Some apologist scholars have struggled to answer this question because they are overanalyzing instead of just looking for the answer in God's Word. Therefore, if we are to answer this question, we must go back to Adam and Eve at the time of the first sin. Many have read this account, but I will list the texts as a refresher.

Genesis 2:17 Updated American Standard Version (UASV)

¹⁷ but from the tree of the knowledge of good and evil you shall not eat,[159] for in the day that you eat from it you shall surely die."[160]

Genesis 3:1-5 Updated American Standard Version (UASV)

¹ Now the serpent was more crafty than any beast of the field which Jehovah God had made. And he said to the woman, "Did God actually say, 'You[161] shall not eat of any tree in the garden'?" ² And the woman said to the serpent, "From the fruit of the trees of the garden we may eat, ³ but from the

---

[159] Lit *eat from it*

[160] Lit *dying you* [singular] *shall die.* Heb *moth tamuth*; the first reference to death in the Scriptures

[161] In Hebrew *you* is plural in verses 1–5

tree that is in the midst of the garden, God said, 'You shall not eat from it, nor shall you touch it, lest you die.'" [4] And the serpent said to the woman, "You shall not surely die. [5] For God knows that when you eat of it your eyes will be opened, and you will be like God, knowing good and evil." knowing good and evil.

Later Bible texts establish Satan the Devil as the one using a serpent as his mouthpiece like a ventriloquist would a dummy. Anyway, take note that Satan contradicts the clear statement that God made to Adam at Genesis 2:17, "you will not surely die." Backing up a little, we see Satan asking an inferential question, "Did God actually say, 'You shall not eat of any tree in the garden'?" First, he is overstating what he knows to be true, not "any tree," just one tree. Second, Satan is inferring, 'I can't believe that God would say . . . how dare he say such.' Notice too that Eve has been told so thoroughly about the tree that she even goes beyond what Adam told her, not just that you 'do not eat from it,' no, 'you do not even touch it!' Then, Satan out and out lied and slandered God as a liar, saying that 'they would not die.' To make matters much worse, he infers that God is withholding good from them, and by rebelling, they would be better off, being like God, 'knowing good and bad.' This latter point is not knowledge of; it is the self-sovereignty of choosing good and bad for oneself and act of rebellion for created creatures. What was symbolized by the tree is well expressed in a footnote on Genesis 2:17, in The Jerusalem Bible (1966):

> This knowledge is a privilege which God reserves to himself and which man, by sinning, is to lay hands on, 3:5, 22. Hence it does not mean omniscience, which fallen man does not possess; nor is it moral discrimination, for unfallen man already had it and God could not refuse it to a rational being. It is the power of deciding for himself what is good and what is evil and of acting accordingly, a claim to complete moral independence by which man refuses to recognize his status as a created being. The first sin was an attack on God's sovereignty, a sin of pride.

The Issues at Hand

(1) Satan called God a liar and said he was not to be trusted regarding the life or death issue.

(2) Satan's challenge took into question the right and legitimacy of God's rightful place as the Universal Sovereign.

(3) Satan also suggested that people would remain obedient to God only as long as they submit to God to their benefit.

(4) Satan all but said that humankind could walk on their own. There was no need for dependence on God.

(5) Satan argued that man could be like God, choosing for himself what is right and wrong.

(6) Satan claimed that God's way of ruling was not in the best interests of humans, and they could do better without God.

Job 1:6-11 Updated American Standard Version (UASV)

6 Now there was a day when the sons of God came to present themselves before Jehovah, and Satan also came among them. **7** Jehovah said to Satan, "From where do you come?" Then Satan answered Jehovah and said, "From roaming about on the earth and walking around on it." **8** Jehovah said to Satan, "Have you considered my servant Job? For there is no one like him on the earth, a blameless and upright man, fearing God and turning away from evil." **9** Then Satan answered Jehovah, "Does Job fear God for nothing? **10** Have you not made a hedge about him and his house and all that he has, on every side? You have blessed the work of his hands, and his possessions have increased in the land. **11** But put forth your hand now and touch all that he has; he will surely curse you to your face."

Job 2:4-5 Updated American Standard Version (UASV)

4 Satan answered Jehovah and said, "Skin for skin! Yes, all that a man has he will give for his life. **5** However, put forth your hand now, and touch his bone and his flesh; he will curse you to your face."

This general reference to "a man," as opposed to explicitly naming Job, suggests that all men [and women] will only obey God when things are good, but when the slightest difficulty arises, he will not obey. If you were put to the test, would you prove your love for your heavenly Father and show that you preferred His rule to that of any other?

God Settles the Issues

There is one thing that Satan did not challenge, namely, the power of God. Satan did not suggest that God was unable to destroy him as an opposer. However, he did challenge God's way of ruling, not His right to rule. Therefore, a moral issue must be settled.

An illustration of how God chose to deal with the issue can be demonstrated in human terms. A neighbor down the street slandered a man who had a son and daughter. The slanderer said that he was not a good father, i.e., he withheld good from his children and was so overbearing, to the point of being abusive. The slanderer stated that the children would be better off

133

without their father. He further argued that the children had no real love for their father and only obeyed him because of the food and shelter. How should the father deal with these false, i.e., slanderous accusations? If he were to go down the road and pummel the slanderer, it would only validate the lies, making the neighbors believe the accuser is telling the truth.

The answer lies within his family, as they can serve as his witnesses. (Pro 27:11; Isa 43:10) If the children stay obedient and grow to be successful adults, turning out to be loving, caring, honest people with spotless character, it proves the accusations false. If the children accept the lies and rebel and become despicable, it further validates that they would have been better off by staying with the father. This is how God chose to deal with the issues. The issues that were raised must be settled beyond all reasonable doubt.

If God had destroyed the rebellious three: Satan, Adam, and Eve; he would not have resolved the issues of

(1) Whether man could walk on his own,

(2) if he would be better off without his Creator,

(3) if God's rulership were not best, and

(4) if God were hiding good things from man.

(5) In addition, there was an audience of untold billions of angelic spirit creatures looking on.

If God destroyed things without settling, these spirit persons would follow God out of dreadful fear, not love, fear of displeasing God. Moreover, say He did kill them and start over, and ten thousand years down the road (with billions of humans now on earth), the issues were raised again, He would have to destroy billions of people again, and again, and again all throughout time, until these issues were laid to rest.

What God has done is, allow time to pass and the issues to be resolved. Man thought he was better off without God and could walk on his own. In addition, man has attempted every kind of rulership imaginable, and one must ask, 'have they proven themselves better than rulership under the sovereignty of their Creator?' (Proverbs 1:30-33; Isaiah 59:4, 8) Sadly, the issues must be taken up to the brink of destroying man. (Rev 11:18) otherwise, the argument would be that if given enough time, they could have turned things around. If man goes up to the point of destroying himself and Armageddon comes at the last minute, it will have set a case law, solved the issue, and the Bible can serve as the example forever. If the issues of God's sovereignty or the loyalty of His created creatures, angelic or human, is ever questioned again, we would have the Holy Bible that will serve as a law established based on previous verdicts of not guilty. Please see below.

What Have the Results Been?

(1) God does not cause evil and suffering. Romans 9:14.

(2) The fact that God has allowed evil, pain, and suffering has shown that independence from God has not brought about a better world. Jeremiah 8:5, 6, 9.

(3) God's permission of evil, pain, and suffering has also proved that Satan has not been able to turn all humans away from God. Exodus 9:16; 1 Samuel 12:22; Hebrews 12:1.

(4) The fact that God has permitted evil, pain, and suffering to continue has provided proof that only God, the Creator, has the capability and the right to rule over humankind for their eternal blessing and happiness. Ecclesiastes 8:9.

(5) Satan has been the god of this world since the sin in Eden (over 6,000 years), and how has that worked out for man, and what has been the result of man's course of independence from God and his rule? Matthew 4:8-9; John 16:11; 2 Corinthians 4:3-4; 1 John 5:19; Psalm 127:1.

Satan's impact on the earth's activities has carried with it conflict, evil, and death, and his rulership has been by means of deception, power, and his own self-interest. He has demonstrated himself as an unfit ruler of everything. Therefore, God is now completely vindicated in putting an end to this corrupted rebel along with all who have shared in his evil deeds. – Romans 16:20.

To resolve all the issues raised by Satan, God has tolerated evil, sickness, pain, suffering, and death until our day. We are self-centered in thinking that this has only pained us. Imagine that you are holding a rope on a sinking ship that 20 other men, women, and children are clinging to when your child loses her grip and falls into the ocean. You can either hold the rope, saving 20 people, or you can let go and attempt to rescue your daughter. God has been watching the suffering of billions from the day of Adam and Eve's sin. Moreover, it has been His great love for us, which causes Him to cling to the rope of issues, saving us from a future of repeated issues. Nevertheless, he will not allow this evil to remain forever. He has set a fixed time when He will end this wicked system of Satan's rule.

Daniel 11:27 Updated American Standard Version (UASV)

²⁷ As for both kings, their heart will be inclined to do what is evil, and they will speak lies to each other at the same table; but it will not succeed, for the end is still to come <u>at the appointed time</u>.

135

Unlike what many people of the world may think (the world that lies in the hands of Satan), being obedient to God is not difficult. We simply must set our pride aside and accept that the wisdom of God is so far greater than our own, and accept that He has worked for the good of obedient humankind, as He loves each one of us.

Matthew 7:21 Updated American Standard Version (UASV)

[21] "Not everyone who says to me, 'Lord, Lord,' will enter the kingdom of heaven, but <u>the one who does the will of my Father</u> who is in heaven.

1 John 2:15-17 Updated American Standard Version (UASV)

[15] Do not love the world or the things in the world. If anyone loves the world, the love of the Father is not in him. [16] For all that is in the world, the lust of the flesh and the lust of the eyes and the boastful pride of life, is not from the Father, but is from the world. [17] The world is passing away, and its lusts; but the one who does the will of God remains forever.

As Christians, there is a love we must not have. We must 'not love the world or anything in it.' Instead, we need to keep from becoming infected by the corruption of unrighteous human society that is alienated from God and must not breathe in its mental disposition or be moved by its sinful dominant attitude. (Ephesians 2:1-2; James 1:27) If we were to have the views of those in the world who oppose God, "the love of the Father" would not be in us. – James 4:4.

An Overview

Was Satan Punished?

Yes.

COMMON QUESTION: Why did God not destroy the Satan, Adam, and Eve right away?

I would follow up with what would have happened if God had chosen that path. Hundreds of billions of angels with free will were watching, and they knew of the issues raised. What would their love of God have been like if God did not address the issues raised? Was Satan right? Was God lying? Would free will creatures, spirits and humans, be better off? Will God just destroy us over anything? First, the spirit creatures would have followed God out of dreadful fear, rather than fear of displeasing the one they loved so much up to that point, like a child to a parent. Second, what happens if the issue is raised a hundred thousand years after a restart and there are 30 billion perfect humans on the planet? Would God simply destroy everyone again

136

and start over. Do we think it wise that he does this reboot every time or was it not better that he settled the issue once and for all?

POINT: Satan raised Issues of sovereignty in the Garden of Eden.

POINT: Can humans walk on their own; do they really need their Creator? Are they better off without God?

POINT: Was God lying and withholding?

When a teenager becomes a rebel in our house, we have a choice: (1) severe punishment or (2) teach them an object lesson.

HUMANS AND ANGELS are a created product no different than a car coming off of an assembly line, i.e., (1) they owe their existence to their creator and (2) they were created to function based on the design of the creator. If we take a ford escort and treat it like a heavy-duty four-wheel-drive truck and go off-roading (not what the car was designed to do), what will happen?

God wisely chose to teach both angels and humans an object lesson. Neither was designed to walk on their own. Both angels and humans were given relative freedom (under the sovereignty of God), not absolute freedom. They were not designed to choose what is right and what is wrong on their own. They were given God's moral standards by way of an internal conscience. How can we tell a rebel that we do not have absolute freedom, we are better off under the umbrella of our creator's sovereignty, we cannot walk on our own? They will just reject it as a rebel teenager would.

OBJECT LESSON: We let them learn from their choice, no matter how painful it is, and hard love means that we do not step in until the lesson is fully learned. Humankind was essentially told, "Oh, you think you can walk on your own, well go ahead, we will see how that works out." After six-thousand-years, God could actually use a common saying among young people today: "How is that absolute freedom working out for you?"

When will the lesson fully be learned? Humankind will walk right up to the very edge of the cliff of killing themselves, actually falling over, when God will step in and stop the object lesson. To stop it anytime before will cause doubts. If it had been stopped a century ago, the argument would have been; God simply stepped in before we got to the scientific age because he knew we were going to find true peace and security, along with something to give us eternal life. However, if humanity has actually fallen over the edge of the cliff and the destruction of us is definite, and God steps in, there is no argument that can be raised, the object lesson is learned.

Why Was Satan Not Kicked Out of Heaven Right Away?

Satan stayed in his realm, just as humans stayed in theirs. God changed nothing right away because he would have been accused of adjusting the pieces on the chessboard to get the desired outcome, i.e., cheating. When will Satan be kicked out of heaven? Satan and the Demons lost access to the person of God long ago, and they lost some of their powers, such as being able to materialize in human form, like they did when they took human women for themselves at the flood, producing the Nephilim.

Satan would be thrown to the earth very shortly before the end of his age of rulership, when "he knows that his time is short." (Rev 12:9-12) This, then, means that Satan will be thrown from heaven, likely sometime before the Great Tribulation and Christ's return. Revelation 12:12 says, "'Therefore, rejoice, O heavens and you who dwell in them! But woe to you, O earth and sea, for the devil has come down to you in great wrath because he knows that his time is short!'"

Notice that it is at a time when "Satan knows that his time is short!" What comes next for Satan? He will be abyssed, thrown into a super-maximum-security prison for a thousand years (for lack of a better way to explain it), while Jesus fixes all that Satan did. After the thousand years, he will be let loose for a little while, and he will tempt perfect humans, and sadly some will fall away. In the end, Satan and those humans will be destroyed, and Jesus will hand the kingdom back over to the father.

Bibliography

Akin, Daniel L. *The New American Commentary: 1, 2, 3 John*. Nashville, TN: Broadman & Holman , 2001.

Akin, Daniel L., David P. Nelson, and Jr. Peter R. Schemm. *A Theology for the Church*. Nashville: B & H Publishing, 2007.

Aland, Kurt and Barbara. *The Text of the New Testament*. Grand Rapids: Eerdmans, 1987.

Alden, Robert L. *Job, The New American Commentary, vol. 11* . Nashville: Broadman & Holman Publishers, 2001.

Anders, Max. *Holman New Testament Commentary: vol. 8, Galatians, Ephesians, Philippians, Colossians*. Nashville, TN: Broadman & Holman Publishers, 1999.

—. *Holman Old Testament Commentary - Proverbs* . Nashville: B&H Publishing, 2005.

Anders, Max, and Doug McIntosh. *Holman Old Testament Commentary - Deuteronomy*. Nashville: B&H Publishing, 2009.

Anders, Max, and Steven Lawson. *Holman Old Testament Commentary - Psalms: 11*. Grand Rapids: B&H Publishing, 2004.

Anders, Max, and Trent Butler. *Holman Old Testament Commentary: Isaiah*. Nashiville, TN: B&H Publishing, 2002.

Anderson, Neil T. *Discipleship Counseling: The Complete Guide to Helping Others: Walk in Freedon and Gow in Christ*. Ventura: Regal Books, 2003.

Andrews, Edward D. *BOOKS OF 2 JOHN 3 JOHN and JUDE CPH New Testament Commentary*. Cambridge: Christian Publishing House, 2013.

—. *FOR AS I THINK IN MY HEART—SO I AM: Combining Biblical Counseling with Cognitive Behavioral Therapy*. Cambridge: Christian Publishing House, 2013.

—. *PUT OFF THE OLD PERSON WITH ITS PRACTICES And Put On the New Person*. Cambridge: Christian Publishing House, 2014.

—. *The Text of the New Testament: A Beginner's Guide to New Testament Textual Criticism*. Cambridge, OH: Bible-Translation.Net Books, 2012.

Andrews, Stephen J, and Robert D Bergen. *Holman Old Testament Commentary: 1-2 Samuel*. Nashville: Broadman & Holman, 2009.

Archibald, Hunter, H. *Interpreting the Parables. London:SCM*. Philadephia: Westminster, 1980.

Arndt, William, Frederick W. Danker, and Walter Bauer. *A Greek-English Lexicon of the New Testament and Other Early Christian Literature. 3rd ed.* . Chicago: University of Chicago Press, 2000.

Arnold, Clinton E. *Zondervan Illustrated Bible Backgrounds Commentary Volume 2: John, Acts.* . Grand Rapids, MI: Zondervan, 2002.

—. *Zondervan Illustrated Bible Backgrounds Commentary Volume 3: Romans to Philemon.* Grand Rapids: Zondervan, 2002.

—. *Zondervan Illustrated Bible Backgrounds Commentary Volume 4: Hebrews to Revelation.* Grand Rapids, MI: Zondervan, 2002.

—. *Zondervan Illustrated Bible Backgrounds Commentary: Matthew, Mark, Luke, vol. 1.* Grand Rapids, MI: Zondervan, 2002.

Baer, Daniel. *The Unquenchable Fire.* Maitland, FL: Xulon Press, 2007.

Barclay, William. *The Letter to the Hebrews (New Daily Study Bible).* Louisville, KY: Westminster John Knox Press, 2002.

Barker, Kenneth L., and Waylon Bailey. *The New American Commentary: vol. 20, Micah, Nahum, Habakkuk, Zephaniah.* Nashville, TN: Broadman & Holman Publishers, 2001.

Barnett, Paul. *The Birth of Christianity: The First Twenty Years (After Jesus, Vol. 1)* . Grand Rapids, MI: Wm. B. Eerdmans , 2005.

Barry, John D., and Lazarus Wentz. *The Lexham Bible Dictionary.* Bellingham, WA: Logos Bible Software, 2012.

Benner, David G. *Strategic Pastoral Counseling: A Short-Term Structural Model.* Grand Rapids: Baker Academic, 1992, 2003.

Benner, David G., and Peter C Hill. *Baker Encyclopedia of Psychology and Counseling (Second Edition).* Grand Rapids: Baker Books, 1985, 1999.

Bercot, David W. *A Dictionary of Early Christian Beliefs.* Peabody: Hendrickson, 1998.

Bergen, Robert D. *The New American Commentary: 1-2 Samuel.* Nashville: Broadman & Holman, 1996.

Black, David Alan. *IT"S STILL GREEK TO ME: An Easy-to-Understand Guide t Intermediate Greek.* Grand Rapids: Baker Books, 1998.

Bland, Dave. *The College Press NIV Commentary: Proverbs, Ecclesiastes & Song of Songs,* . Joplin: College Press Pub. Co., 2002.

Blenkinsopp, Joseph. *Isaiah 56-66: A New Translation with Introduction and Commentary*. New York: Anchor Bible, 2003.

Blomberg, Craig. *The New American Commentary: Matthew*. Nashville, TN: Broadman & Holman Publishers, 1992.

Boa, Kenneth, and William Kruidenier. *Holman New Testament Commentary: Romans*. Nashville: Broadman & Holman, 2000.

—. *Holman New Testament Commentary: Romans, Vol. 6*. Nashville, TN: Broadman & Holman, 2000.

Boisen, Sean, Mark Keaton, Jeremy Thompson, and David Witthoff. *Bible Sense Lexicon*. Bellingham: Lexham Press, June 25, 2014.

Boles, Kenneth L. *The College Press NIV commentary: Galatians & Ephesians*. Joplin, MO: College Press, 1993.

Borchert, Gerald L. *The New American Commentary: John 1-11* . Nashville, TN: Broadman & Holman Publishers, 2001.

Borchert, Gerald L. *The New American Commentary vol. 25B, John 12–21*. Nashville: Broadman & Holman Publishers, 2002.

Boyd, Gregory A, and Paul R Eddy. *Across the Spectrum [Secon Edition]*. Grand Rapids: Baker Academic, 2002, 2009.

Brand, Chad, Charles Draper, and England Archie. *Holman Illustrated Bible Dictionary: Revised, Updated and Expanded*. Nashville, TN: Holman, 2003.

Bratcher, Robert G., and Howard Hatton. *A Handbook on the Revelation to John*. New York: United Bible Societies, 1993.

Breneman, Mervin. *The New American Commentary, vol. 10, Ezra, Nehemiah, Esther*. Nashville: Broadman & Holman Publishers, 1993.

Briley, Terry R. *The College Press NIV Commentary: Isaiah*. Joplin, MO: ollege Press Pub, 2000.

Brisco, Thomas V. *Holman Bible Atlas, Holman Reference*. Nashville, TN: Broadman & Holman Publishers, 1998.

Bromiley, Geoffrey W. *The International Standard Bible Encyclopedia (Vol. 1-4)*. Grand Rapids, MI: William B. Eerdmans Publishing Co., 1986.

Bromiley, Geoffrey W., and Gerhard Friedrich. *Theological Dictionary of the New Testament, ed. Gerhard Kittel, vol. 4*. Grand Rapids, MI: Eerdmans, 1964-.

Brooks, James A. *The New American Commentary: Mark (Volume 23)*. Nashville: Broadman & Holman Publishers, 1992.

Bruce, F. F. *The New International Commentary on the New Testament: The Epistle to the Hebrews (Revised)*. Grand Rapids, MI: William B. Eermans Publishing Company, 1990.

Buter, Trent C. *Holman New Testament Commentary: Luke*. Nashville, TN: Broadman & Holman Publishers, 2000.

Butler, Trent C. *Holman New Testament Commentary: Luke*. Nashville, TN: Broadman & Holman Publishers, 2000.

Butler, Trent C. *Holman Old Testament Commentary - Hosea, Joel, Amos, Obadiah, Jonah, Micah* . Nashville: Broadman & Holman Publishers, 2005.

Caba, Tedl et al.,. *The Apologetics Study Bible: Real Questions, Straight Answers, Stronger Faith*. Nashville: Holman Bible Publishers, 2007.

Calloway, Brent A. *THE BOOK OF JAMES: CPH CHRISTIAN LIVING COMMENTARY*. Cambridge: Chriwstian Publishing House, 2015.

Carpenter, Eugene E., and Philip W Comfort. *The Holman Treasury of Key Bible Words: 200 Greek and 200 Hebrew Words Defined and Explained*. Nashville: Broadman & Holman Publishers, 2000.

Carson, D. A, and Douglas J Moo. *An Introduction to the New Testament*. Grand Rapids, MI: Zondervan, 2005.

Carson, D. A. *New Bible Commentary: 21st Century Edition. 4th ed*. Downers Grove: Inter-Varisity Press, 1994.

Clinton, Tim, and George Ohlschlager. *Competent Christian Counseling; Volume One: Foundations and Practice of Compassionate Soul Care*. Colorado Springs, CO: WaterBrook Press, 2008.

Cole, R. Dennis. *THE NEW AMERICAN COMMENTARY: Volume 3b Numbers*. Nashville: Broadman & Holman Publishers, 2000.

Comfort, Philip. *Encounterring the Manuscripts: An Introduction to New Testament Paleography and Textual Criticism*. Nashville: Broadman & Holman, 2005.

Comfort, Philip W. *New Testament Text and Translation Commentary*. Carol Stream: Tyndale House Publishers, 2008.

Comfort, Philip, and David Barret. *The Text of the Earliest New Testament Greek Manuscripts*. Wheaton: Tyndale House Publishers, 2001.

Cooper, Lamar Eugene. *The New American Commentary, Ezekiel, vol. 17.* Nashville, TN: Broadman & Holman Publishers, 1994.

Cooper, Rodney. *Holman New Testament Commentary: Mark.* Nashville: Broadman & Holman Publishers, 2000.

Cottrell, Peter, and Maxwell Turner. *Linguistics and Biblical Interpretation.* Downers Grove: InterVarsity Press, 1989.

Cruse, C. F. *Eusebius' Eccliatical History.* Peabody, MA: Hendrickson, 1998.

Davis, Christopher A. *THE COLLEGE PRESS NIV COMMENTARY: Revelation.* Joplin: College Press Publishing Co., 2000.

Dockery, David S, and George H. Guthrie. *The Holman Guide to Interpreting the Bible.* Nashville: Broadman & Holman Publishers, 2004.

Dockery, David S. *HOLMAN CONCISE BIBLE COMMENTARY Simple, straightforward commentary on every book of the Bible.* Nashville: Broadman & Holman, 1998.

Dockery, David S., and Trent C. Church, Christopher L. Butler. *Holman Bible Handbook* . Nashville, TN: Holman Bible Publishers, 1992.

Easley, Kendell H. *Holman New Testament Commentary, vol. 12, Revelation.* (Nashville, TN: Broadman & Holman Publishers, 1998.

Easton, M. G. *Easton's Bible Dictionary.* Oak Harbor, WA: Logos Research Systems, 1996, c1897.

Edwards, Tyron. *A Dictionary of Thoughts.* Detroit: F. B. Dickerson Company, 1908.

Ellingworth, Paul. *The Epistle to the Hebrews: A Commentary on the Greek Text.* Grand Rapids, MI: W.B. Eerdmans, 1993.

Elliott, Charles. *Delineation Of Roman Catholicism: Drawn From The Authentic And Acknowledged Standards Of the Church Of Rome, Volume II.* New York: George Lane, 1941.

Elwell, Walter A. *Baker Encyclopedia of the Bible.* Grand Rapids: Baker Book House, 1988.

—. *Evangelical Dictionary of Theology (Second Edition).* Grand Rapids: Baker Academic, 2001.

Elwell, Walter A, and Philip Wesley Comfort. *Tyndale Bible Dictionary.* Wheaton, Ill: Tyndale House Publishers, 2001.

Enns, Paul P. *The Moody Handbook of Theology.* Chicago: Moody Press, 1997.

Erickson, Millard J. "Biblical Inerrancy: the last twenty-five years." *Journal of the Evangelical Theological Society*, 1982: 387-394.

—. *Introducing Christian Doctrine.* Grand Rapids: Baker Book House, 1992.

Erickson, Millard J. *The Concise Dictionary of Christian Theology.* Wheaton: Crossway Books, 2001.

Erickson, Milliard J. *Christian Theology (Third Edition).* Grand Rapids, MI: Baker Academic, 2013.

Ferguson, Everett. *Backgrounds of Early Christianity.* Grand Rapids, MI: Wm. B. Eerdmans, 2003.

—. *Baptism in the Early Church: History, Theology, and Liturgy in the First Five Centuries.* Grand Rapids, MI: Eerdmans, 2009.

Freedman, David Noel, Allen C. Myers, and Astrid B. Beck. *Eerdmans Dictionary of the Bible.* Grand Rapids, Mich.: W.B. Eerdmans , 2000.

Friberg, Timothy, Barbara Friberg, and Neva F. Miller. *Analytical Lexicon of the Greek New Testament.* Grand Rapids: Baker Books, 2000.

—. *Analytical Lexicon of the Greek New Testament, Baker's Greek New Testament Library.* Grand Rapids, MI: Baker Books, 2000.

Galli, Mark, and Ted Olsen. *131 Christians Everyone Should Know .* Nashville, TN : Broadman & Holman Publishers, 2000.

Gangel, Kenneth O. *Holman New Testament Commentary: Acts.* Nashville, TN: Broadman & Holman Publishers, 1998.

Gangel, Kenneth O. *Holman New Testament Commentary, vol. 4, John .* Nashville, TN: Broadman & Holman Publishers, 2000.

—. *Holman Old Testament Commentary: Daniel.* Nashville: Broadman & Holman Publishers, 2001.

Garland, David E. *1 Corinthians, Baker Exegetical Commentary on the New Testament.* Grand Rapids, MI: : Baker Academic, 2003.

Garrett, Duane A. *Proverbs, Ecclesiastes, Song of Songs, The New American Commentary, vol. 14.* Nashville: Broadman & Holman Publishers, 1993.

—. *The New American Commentary: Vol. 14 (Proverbs, Ecclesiastes, Song of Songs).* Nashville: Broadman & Holman Publishers, 1993.

Geisler, Norman L. *Systematic Theology in One Volume.* Minneapolis, MN: Bethany House, 2011.

Geisler, Norman L, and William E Nix. *A General Introduction to the Bible.* Chicago: Moody Press, 1996.

George, Timothy. *The New American Commentary: Galatians* . Nashville, TN: Broadman & Holman Publishers, 2001.

Green, Joel B, Scot McKnight, and Howard Marshall. *Dictionary of Jesus and the Gospels.* Downers Grove, IL: InterVarsity Press, 1992.

Greenlee, J Harold. *Introduction to New Testament Textual Criticism.* Peabody: Hendrickson, 1995.

Grudem, Wayne. *Making Sense of the Bible: One of Seven Parts from Grudem's Systematic Theology (Making Sense of Series).* Grand Rapids: Zondervan, 2011.

Gruden, Wayne. *Are Miraculous Gifts for Today?: 4 Views (Counterpoints: Bible and Theology).* Grand Rapids: Zondervan, 2011.

Guralnik, David B. *Webster's New World Dictionary, 2d college ed.* New York, NY: Simon and Schuster, 1984.

Guthrie, Donald. *Introduction to the New Testament (Revised and Expanded).* Downers Grove, IL: InterVarsity Press, 1990.

Guthrie, George H. *The NIV Application Commentary: Hebrews.* Grand Rapids, MI: Zondervan, 1998.

Harris, Robert Laird, Gleason Leonard Archer, and Bruce K Waltke. *Theological Wordbook of the Old Testament.* Chicago: Moody Press, 1999, c1980.

Hastings, James, John A Selbie, and John C Lambert. *A Dictionary of Christ and the Gospels.* New York, NY: Charles Scribner's Sons, 1907.

Hendriksen, William. *Baker New Testament Commentary: Matthew.* Grand Rapids: Baker Book House, 1973.

Hill, Jonathan. *Zondervan Handbook to the History of Christianity.* Oxford: Lion, 2006.

Hoerth, Alfred. *Archaeology and the Old Testament.* Grand Rapids: Baker, 1998.

Holmes, Michael W. *The Apostolic Fathers: Greek Texts and English Translations.* Grand Rapids: Baker Academics, 2007.

House, Paul R. *The New American Commentary: 2 Kings* . Nashville: Broadman & Holman Publishers, 2001.

Johnson, W. Ronald. *How Would They Hear if We Do Not Listen?* Nashville: Broadman & Holman Publishers, 1994.

Keener, Craig S. *The IVP Bible Background Commentary: New Testament*. Downer Groves, IL: InterVarsity Press, 1993.

Keil, Carl Friedrich, and Franz Delitzsch. *Commentary on the Old Testament*. Peabody, MA: Hendrickson, 2002.

Kistemaker, Simon J. *Baker New Testament Commentary: Hebrews*. Grand Rapids: Baker Books, 1984.

Kistemaker, Simon J, and Hendriksen William. *New Testament Commentary: Exposition of the Gospel According to Luke*. Grand Rapids: Baker Book House, 1953-2001.

Kistemaker, Simon J, and William Hendriksen. *New Testament Commentary: Exposition of Paul's Epistle to the Romans* . Grand Rapids, MI : Baker Book House , 1953-2001.

—. *New Testament Commentary: vol. 15, Exposition of Hebrews*. Grand Rapids: Baker Book House, 1953-2001.

—. *New Testament Commentary: vol. 19, Exposition of the Second Epistle to the Corinthians*. Grand Rapids, MI:: Baker Book House, 1953-2001.

Kistemaker, Simon J., and William Hendriksen. *Exposition of the First Epistle to the Corinthians, vol. 18, New Testament Commentary*. Grand Rapids, MI: Baker Book House, 1953–2001.

Kittel, Gerhard, Gerhard Friedrich, and Geoffrey William Bromiley. *Theological Dictionary of the New Testament*. Grand Rapids: Eerdmans, 1995, c1985.

Knight, George W. *The Layman's Bible Handbook*. Uhrichsville: Barbour Publishing, 2003.

Kollar, Charles Allen. *Solution-Focused Pastoral Counseling: An Effective Short-Term Approach for Getting People Back on Track*. Grand Rapids: Zondervan, 1997.

Lange, J. P. *Commentary of the Holy Scriptures: Revelation*. New York: Scribner's, 1872.

Larson, Knute. *Holman New Testament Commentary, vol. 9, I & II Thessalonians, I & II Timothy, Titus, Philemon*. Nashville, TN: Broadman & Holman Publishers, 2000.

Lea, Thomas D, and David Allen Black. *The New Testament: Its Background Message. 2d ed*. Nashville, TN: B & H Academic, 2003.

Lea, Thomas D. *Holman New Testament Commentary: Hebrews, James*. Nashville, TN: Broadman & Holman Publishers, 1999.

——. *Holman New Testament Commentary: Vol. 10, Hebrews, James.* Nashville, TN: Broadman & Holman Publishers, 1999.

Lea, Thomas D., and Hayne P. Griffin. *The New American Commentary, vol. 34, 1, 2 Timothy, Titus.* Nashville: Broadman & Holman Publishers, 1992.

Lightfoot, Neil R. *How We Got the Bible.* Grand Rapids, MI: Baker Books, 1963, 1988, 2003.

Lukaszewski, Albert L., Mark Dubis, and Ted J Blakley. *The Lexham Syntactic Greek New Testament.* Bellingham: Logos Bible Software, 2013.

MacArthur, John. *Counseling: How to Counsel Biblically.* Nashville, TN: Thomas Nelson, Inc., 2005.

Macarthur, John. *Fool's Gold: Discerning Truth in an Age of Error.* Wheaton: Crossway Books, 2005.

MacArthur, John. *Pastoral Ministry: How to Shepherd Biblically.* Nashville: Thomas Nelson, 2005.

——. *The MacArthur Bible Commentary.* Nashville: Thomas Nelson, 2005.

Marshall, Alfred. *THE NASB-NIV INTERLINEAR GREEK-ENGLISH NEW TESTAMENT.* Grand Rapids: Zondervan, 1993.

Martin, D Michael. *The New American Commentary 33 1, 2 Thessalonians .* Nashville, TN: Broadman & Holman, 2001, c1995 .

Martin, Glen S. *Holman Old Testament Commentary: Numbers.* Nashville: Broadman & Holman Publishers, 2002.

Mathews, K. A. *The New American Commentary vol. 1A, Genesis 1-11:26 .* Nashville: Broadman & Holman Publishers, 2001.

Matthews, K. A. *The New American Commentary Vol. 1B, Genesis 11:27-50:26.* Nashville: Broadman and Holman Publishers, 2001.

McMinn, Mark R. *Psychology, Theology, and Spirituality in Christian Counseling (AACC Library).* Carol Stream, IL: Tyndale House Publishers, 2010.

McRaney, William. *The Art of Personal Evangelism.* Nashville: Broadman & Holman, 2003.

Melick, Richard R. *The New American Commentary: Philippians, Colossians, Philemon, electronic ed., Logos Library System.* Nashville: Broadman & Holman Publishers, 2001.

——. *The New American Commentary: vol. 32, Philippians, Colissians, Philemon.* Nashville, TN : Broadman & Holman Publishers, 2001.

Metzger, Bruce M. *The Text of the New Testament: Its Transmission, Corruption, and Transmission.* New York: Oxford University Press, 1964, 1968, 1992.

Metzger, Bruce M. *A Textual Commentary on the Greek New Testament.* New York: United Bible Society, 1994.

Microsoft. *Encarta ® World English Dictionary.* Redmond: Microsoft Corporation, 1998-2010.

Miller, Stephen R. *The New American Commentary: Volume 18 Daniel.* Nashville: Broadman & Holman Publishers, 1994.

Mirriam-Webster, Inc. *Mirriam-Webster's Collegiate Dictionary. Eleventh Edition.* Springfield: Mirriam-Webster, Inc., 2003.

Morris, Leon. *The Gospel According to Matthew.* Grand Rapids, MI: Inter-Varsity Press, 1992.

—. *Tyndale New Testament Commentaries: Revelation.* Grand Rapids: William Eerdmans Publishing Company, 1987.

Mounce, Robert H. *Romans: The New American Commentary 27.* Nashville: Broadman & Holman, 2001, c1995.

Mounce, Robert H. *The New American Commentary: Vol. 27 Romans.* Nashville, TN: Broadman & Holman Publishers, 2001.

Mounce, Robert. *Robert Mounce, The New International Commentary of the New Testament: The Book of Revelation.* Grand Rapids: William Eerdmans Publishing Company, 1977.

Mounce, William D. *Mounce's Complete Expository Dictionary of Old & New Testament Words.* Grand Rapids, MI: Zondervan, 2006.

Mounce, William D. *Basics of Biblical Greek Grammar.* Grand Rapids: Zonervan, 2009.

Myers, Allen C. *The Eerdmans Bible Dictionary .* Grand Rapids, Mich: Eerdmans, 1987.

Niessen, Richard. "The virginity of the `almah in Isaiah 7:14." *Bibliotheca Sacra 137* , 1980: 133-50.

Osborne, Grant R. *BAKER EXEGETICAL COMMENTARY ON THE NEW TESTAMET: REVELATION.* Grand Rapids, MI: Baker Academic, 2002.

Oswalt, John N. *The NIV Application Commentary: Isaiah.* Grand Rapids, MI: Zondervan, 2003.

Outlaw, W. Stanley. *The Book of Hebrews*. Nashville, TN: Randall House, 2005.

Pink, Arthur Walkington. *An Exposition of Hebrews*. Swengel, PA: Bible Truth Depot, 1954.

Polhill, John B. *The New American Commentary 26: Acts*. Nashville: Broadman & Holman Publishers, 2001.

Pratt Jr, Richard L. *Holman New Testament Commentary: I & II Corinthians, vol. 7*. Nashville: Broadman & Holman Publishers, 2000.

Ramsey, Boniface (Editor). *Manichean Debate (Works of Saint Augustine)*. New City Press: Hyde Park, 2006.

Richards, E. Randolph. *Paul And First-Century Letter Writing: Secretaries, Composition and Collection*. Downers Grove: InterVarsity Press, 2004.

Richardson, Kurt. *The New American Commentary Vol. 36 James*. Nashville: Broadman & Holman Publishers, 1997.

Roberts, Alexander, James Donaldson, and A. Cleveland Coxe. *THE ANTE-NICENE FATHERS 1: The Apostolic Fathers with Justin Martyr and Irenaeus*. Buffalo: The Christian Literature Company, 1885.

Robertson, A. T. *An Introduction to the Textual Criticism of the New Testament*. London: Hodder & Stoughton, 1925.

Robertson, Paul E. "Theology of the Healthy Church." *The Theological Educator: A Journal of Theology and Ministry*, Spring 1998: 45-52.

Robinson, Darrell W. *Total Church Life: How to be a First Century Chrurch*. Nashville, TN: Briadman and Holman, 1997.

Rooker, Mark F. *The New American Commentary, vol. 3A, Leviticus*. Nashville: Broadman & Holman Publishers, 2000.

—. *Holman Old Testament Commentary: Ezekiel*. Nashville: Broadman & Holman Publishers, 2005.

—. *Leviticus: The New American Commentary*. Nashville: Broadman & Holman, 2001.

Schreiner, Thomas R. *The New American Commentary: 1, 2 Peter, Jude*. Nashville: Broadman & Holman, 2003.

Scott, Julius J. Jr. *Jewish Backgrounds of the New Testament*. Grand Rapids, MI: Baker Academic, 1995.

Smith, Gary. *The New American Commentary: Isaiah 1-39, Vol. 15a*. Nashville, TN: B & H Publishing Group, 2007.

—. *The New American Commentary: Isaiah 40-66, Vol. 15b*. Nashville, TN: B&H Publishing, 2009.

Souter, Alexander. *The Text and Canon of the New Testament*. New York: Charles Scribner's Sons, 1913.

Sproul, R. C. *What Is Faith?* Lake Mary: Reformation Trust, 2010.

Stein, Robert H. *A Basic Guide to Interpreting the Bible: Playing by the Rules*. Grand Rapids: Baker Books, 1994.

—. *The New American Commentary: Luke*. Nashville, TN: Broadman & Holman , 2001, c1992.

Stott, John. *The Letters of John (Tyndale New Testament Commentaries)*. Downers Grove: IVP Academic, 2009.

Stuart, Douglas K. *The New American Commentary: An Exegetical Theological Exposition of Holy Scripture EXODUS*. Nashville: Broadman & Holman, 2006.

Swanson, James. *A Dictionary of Biblical Languages - Greek*. Washington: Logos Research Systems, 1997.

Swindoll, Charles R, and Roy B. Zuck. *Understanding Christian Theology*. Nashville, TN: Thomas Nelson Publishers, 2003.

Taylor, Richard A, and Ray E Clendenen. *The New American Commentary: Haggai, Malachi, , vol. 21A* . Nashville, TN: Broadman & Holman Publishers, 2007.

Terry, Milton S. *Biblical Hermeneutics: A Treatise on the Interpretation of the Old and New Testaments*. Grand Rapids: Zondervan, 1883.

Thomas, Robert L. *New American Standard Hebrew-Aramaic and Greek Dictionaries: Updated Edition*. Anaheim: Foundation Publications, Inc., 1998, 1981.

—. *Revelation 1-7: An Exegetical Commentary* . Chicago, IL: Moody Publishers, 1992.

Towns, Elmer L. *Concise Bible Dictrines: Clear, Simple, and Easy-to-Understand Explanations of Bible Doctrines*. Chattanooga: AMG Publishers, 2006.

—. *Theology for Today*. Belmont: Wadsworth Group, 2002.

Tuck, Robert. *A Handbook of Biblical Difficulties: Or Reasonable Solutions of Perplexing Things in Sacred Scriptures (Reprint)*. New York: Bible House, 2012.

Vine, W E. *Vine's Expository Dictionary of Old and New Testament Words.* Nashville: Thomas Nelson, 1996.

Walls, David, and Max Anders. *Holman New Testament Commentary: I & II Peter, I, II & III John, Jude.* Nashville: Broadman & Holman Publishers, 1996.

Walton, John H. *Zondervan Illustrated Bible Backgrounds Commentary (Old Testament) Volume 1: Genesis, Exodus, Leviticus, Numbers, Deuteronomy.* Grand Rapids, MI: Zondervan, 2009.

Walton, John H. "Isaiah 7:14: what's in a name?" *Journal of the Evangelical Theological Society 30,* 1987: 289-306.

—. *Zondervan Illustrated Bible Backgrounds Commentary (Old Testament) Volume 3: 1 & 2 Kings, 1 & 2 Chronicles, Ezra, Nehemiah, Esthe.* Grand Rapids, MI: Zondervan, 2009.

—. *Zondervan Illustrated Bible Backgrounds Commentary (Old Testament) Volume 5: The Minor Prophets, Job, Psalms, Proverbs, Ecclesiastes, Song of Songs.* Grand Rapids, M: Zondervan, 2009.

Walvoord, John F. *Daniel: The Key to Prophetic Revelation.* Chicago, IL: Moody Publishers, 1971, reprint 1989.

Walvoord, John. *The Revelation of Jesus Christ.* Chicago: Moody Press, 1996.

Watson, Richard. *A Biblical and Theological Dictionary: Explanatory of the History, Manners and Customs of the Jews.* New York: Waugh and T. Mason, 1832.

Weatherly, Jon A. *THE COLLEGE PRESS NIV COMMENTARY: 1 & 2 Thessalonians.* Joplin: College Press Publishing Company, 1996.

Weber, Stuart K. *Holman New Testament Commentary, vol. 1, Matthew.* Nashville, TN: Broadman & Holman Publishers, 2000.

Wegner, Paul D. *A Student's Guide to Textual Criticism of the Bible: Its History Methods & Results.* Downers Grove: InterVarsity Press, 2006.

Westcott, B. F., and Hort F. J. A. *The New Testament in the Original Greek, Vol. 2: Introduction, Appendix.* London: Macmillan and Co., 1882.

Whiston, William. *The Works of Josephus.* Peabody, MA: Hendrickson, 1987.

Whitney, Donald S. *Spiritual Disciplines for the Christian Life with Bonus Content (Pilgrimage Growth Guide).* Colorado Springs, CO: Navpress, 1991.

Wilkins, Michael, and Craig A. Evans. *The Gospels and Acts (The Holman Apologetics Commentary on the Bible)*. Nashville: B & H Publishing Group, 2013.

Wolf, Herbert M. "Solution to the Immanuel Prophecy in Isaiah 7:14-8:22." *Journal of Biblical Literature 91* , 1972: 449-56.

Wood, D R W. *New Bible Dictionary (Third Edition)*. Downers Grove: InterVarsity Press, 1996.

Wright, N. T. *Hebrews for Everyone*. London: Westminster John Knox Press, 2003.

Zodhiates, Spiros. *The Complete Word Study Dictionary: New Testament*. Chattanooga: AMG Publishers, 2000, c1992, c1993.

Zuck, Roy B. *Basic Bible Interpretation: A Prafctical Guide to Discovering Biblical Truth*. Colorado Springs: David C. Cook, 1991.

Made in the USA
Coppell, TX
03 September 2023

21153769R00089